GRAVEYARD AND STARFIRE

The Convergence of Aghora and Luciferianism

Jivan Mukta

Mokshadas Press

Being

Chapter 12: Suggested Rituals, Meditations, and Exercises   122

Annotated Bibliography for Further Reading   138

Glossary of Terms   142

INTRODUCTION: THE LEFT-HAND PATHS

In the vast and intricate world of spiritual traditions, the left-hand path stands as both a beacon of transformation and a challenge to the established norms. It is a path that beckons the brave, the curious, and the rebellious, those who seek not just enlightenment but a deeper, more visceral understanding of existence. The left-hand path does not shy away from the shadows; instead, it embraces them, recognizing that within the darkness lies the potential for profound growth, empowerment, and self-realization.

The left-hand path is often defined by its willingness to engage with the taboo, the forbidden, and the terrifying. It is a journey that leads the seeker through the underworld of their psyche, where they must confront their deepest fears, desires, and insecurities. Unlike the right-hand path, which typically emphasizes purity, light, and the renunciation of worldly attachments, the left-hand path sees value in all aspects of existence—light and dark, sacred and profane, life and death. It is a holistic approach to spirituality that acknowledges the necessity of embracing the totality of one's being.

Two traditions that epitomize the essence of the left-hand path are Luciferianism and Aghora. At first glance, these paths may seem worlds apart—Luciferianism, with its roots in Western esotericism and occult philosophy, and Aghora, a radical offshoot of Tantric Hinduism, deeply embedded in the religious and cultural landscape of India. Yet, beneath their cultural differences, these traditions share a profound commonality: both reject the limitations imposed by conventional morality and societal norms, both seek to transcend the ordinary through the extraordinary, and both find power and wisdom in the dark and the forbidden.

Luciferianism is a path that venerates Lucifer not as a demonic figure, but as a symbol of enlightenment, rebellion, and the pursuit of knowledge. It is a tradition that encourages the individual to break free from the chains of conformity, to seek out hidden truths, and to embrace both the light and dark aspects of existence as essential components of self-realization.

Aghora, on the other hand, is a path that challenges the very fabric of societal taboos. Aghoris, the practitioners of this tradition, are known for their radical practices, which include meditating in cremation grounds, using human remains in their rituals, and embracing the impure and the abject as vehicles for spiritual transformation. Aghora is a path of extreme transgression, where the boundaries between life and death, sacred and profane, are deliberately blurred to achieve spiritual liberation.

This book, *Graveyard and Starfire: The Convergence of Aghora and Luciferianism*, seeks to explore the intersections of these two powerful spiritual paths. Through an in-depth examination of their philosophies, rituals, and practices, we will uncover the shared wisdom that lies at the heart of both traditions. This is not merely an academic exploration; it is an invitation to engage with the transformative power of the left-hand path, to embrace the darkness within, and to discover the light that emerges from it.

In the chapters that follow, we will journey through the philosophical foundations of Luciferianism and Aghora, explore their shared rituals and practices, and ultimately discover how these paths lead to enlightenment through the integration of light and dark. Whether you are drawn to the rebellious, self-deifying ethos of Luciferianism or the radical, taboo-breaking practices of Aghora, this book will provide insights and practical guidance for those who seek to walk the left-hand path.

As we embark on this journey, it is important to remember that the left-hand path is not for the faint of heart. It demands courage, introspection, and a willingness to confront the shadow aspects of the self. But for those who are willing to take the plunge, it offers the promise of profound transformation, self-empowerment, and a deeper understanding of the mysteries of existence.

DISCLAIMER AND WARNING

The practices, rituals, and meditations described in this book are derived from esoteric traditions, including Luciferianism and Aghora, which involve profound spiritual exploration, the confrontation of inner darkness, and the challenging of societal norms. These practices are intended for individuals who have a solid foundation in spiritual or occult work and who are prepared for the intense psychological and emotional experiences that may arise.

Potential Dangers:

1. **Psychological and Emotional Impact:** Engaging in shadow work, ego death, and other transformative practices can trigger deep-seated fears, unresolved traumas, and suppressed emotions. It is possible to experience intense psychological or emotional upheaval during or after these practices. Individuals with a

history of mental health issues should exercise caution and consider consulting a qualified mental health professional before engaging in these practices.

2. **Spiritual Imbalance:**
Practices that involve invoking powerful spiritual forces, such as deities or elemental energies, can lead to an imbalance if not approached with respect, preparation, and grounding. The integration of dark or forbidden aspects of the self can be destabilizing if the practitioner is not adequately prepared or supported.

3. **Physical Risks:**
Some rituals may involve fasting, exposure to natural elements, or other physical challenges. These practices should only be undertaken by those in good health and with an understanding of their physical limits. Always ensure that you are physically prepared and that you have taken necessary precautions before engaging in any physically demanding practice.

4. **Ethical and Social Considerations:**
Certain practices, particularly those in

the Aghora tradition, involve actions that may be considered taboo or socially unacceptable. It is essential to consider the ethical implications and potential social consequences of these practices before engaging in them. Practitioners should be mindful of their actions and how they may impact themselves and others.

5. **Spiritual Vulnerability:**
Engaging with the spirit world, whether through invocation, necromancy, or astral projection, can expose practitioners to energies or entities that may be harmful or malevolent. It is crucial to practice proper protective measures, such as banishing rituals and grounding exercises, to ensure spiritual safety.

Legal Disclaimer:

The authors, publishers, and contributors of this book are not responsible for any physical, emotional, psychological, or spiritual harm that may result from the use of the practices described herein. These practices are intended for educational and informational purposes only and should be undertaken at the reader's own risk. Readers are encouraged to approach these practices with caution, respect, and a thorough understanding of their potential risks.

Recommendation:

If you are new to these traditions or unsure of your ability to safely engage in these practices, it is strongly recommended that you seek guidance from an experienced practitioner or mentor. Additionally, consider starting with less intensive practices and gradually working your way up as you build your knowledge, experience, and spiritual resilience.

CHAPTER 1: THE LUCIFERIAN ETHOS

Luciferianism is a spiritual path that is often shrouded in misunderstanding and misconception. To the uninitiated, the very name "Lucifer" conjures images of malevolence, rebellion, and damnation. However, within the context of Luciferian philosophy, Lucifer is not a figure of evil, but rather a symbol of enlightenment, knowledge, and the pursuit of personal sovereignty. Luciferianism is a path that exalts the individual as a potential deity in their own right, urging them to transcend the limitations of conventional morality and to seek the light of wisdom through the embrace of both the light and the dark.

Historical Background of Luciferianism

The origins of Luciferianism are complex and

multifaceted, drawing from various streams of Western esotericism, including Gnosticism, Hermeticism, and the occult traditions of medieval and Renaissance Europe. At its core, Luciferianism is rooted in the figure of Lucifer, a being whose name means "light-bringer" or "morning star." In Christian tradition, Lucifer is often depicted as the fallen angel who defied God and was cast out of heaven. However, in Luciferian thought, this act of defiance is not viewed as a transgression, but as a courageous stand for individual freedom, enlightenment, and the pursuit of forbidden knowledge.

Lucifer's story, as it is traditionally told, is one of rebellion against divine authority. In the book of Isaiah, Lucifer is described as the "son of the morning" who sought to ascend to the throne of God, only to be cast down to the earth for his hubris. This narrative has been interpreted in various ways throughout history, but within Luciferianism, it is seen as an allegory for the human condition—the struggle for self-actualization, the rejection of imposed limitations, and the quest for enlightenment.

The figure of Lucifer has been reinterpreted and reimagined in numerous cultural and literary contexts. In John Milton's *Paradise Lost*, Lucifer is portrayed as a tragic hero, a being of immense power and intellect who challenges the tyranny of heaven in the name of freedom and self-determination. This portrayal has had a significant influence on the development of Luciferian thought, presenting Lucifer not as a symbol of evil, but as an archetype of the enlightened rebel.

In Gnostic traditions, which have also influenced Luciferianism, the figure of the serpent in the Garden of Eden—often associated with Lucifer—is seen as a liberator, offering humanity the knowledge of good and evil, and thereby freeing them from the constraints of ignorance. This Gnostic interpretation emphasizes the role of Lucifer as a bringer of enlightenment, challenging the false authorities and dogmas that seek to keep humanity in darkness.

Over time, these various influences have coalesced into a distinct spiritual tradition known as Luciferianism. It is a path that attracts those who seek to break free from societal constraints, to embrace their own inner power, and to achieve a higher state of consciousness through the integration of both light and dark aspects of the self.

Key Figures and Texts in Luciferian Thought

The development of modern Luciferianism has been shaped by the contributions of several key figures, each of whom has added their own unique perspective to the tradition.

One of the most influential figures in contemporary Luciferianism is Michael W. Ford, an author, occultist, and founder of the Greater Church of Lucifer. Ford's works, such as *The Bible of the Adversary*, *Luciferian Witchcraft*, and *Apotheosis: The Ultimate Beginner's Guide to Luciferianism & the Left-Hand Path*, have become foundational texts for those exploring the Luciferian path. Ford's writings emphasize the importance of self-deification, the pursuit of knowledge, and the integration of light and dark as essential components of spiritual evolution.

Another significant figure is Aleister Crowley, whose Thelemic philosophy shares many parallels with Luciferianism, particularly in its emphasis on individualism, the rejection of conventional morality, and the pursuit of one's true will. Crowley's influence on Luciferianism is profound, particularly in his advocacy for the sovereignty of the individual and the exploration of the darker aspects of the psyche. Although Crowley himself did not identify as a Luciferian, his writings, especially *The Book of the Law* and *Magick Without Tears*, have been highly influential in shaping the modern Luciferian ethos.

John Milton's *Paradise Lost* also stands as a cornerstone of Luciferian literature. Milton's portrayal of Lucifer as a complex and multifaceted character—both noble and flawed, heroic and tragic—has had a lasting impact on the way Lucifer is viewed within the tradition. *Paradise Lost* presents Lucifer as a being who, despite his fall, remains defiant and unyielding in his pursuit of freedom, making him an enduring symbol of resistance against tyranny.

The influence of Gnostic texts, such as *The Apocryphon of John* and *The Gospel of Judas*, cannot be overlooked in the development of Luciferian thought. These texts present alternative narratives that challenge orthodox Christian interpretations, offering a view of Lucifer and other figures associated with darkness as bringers of enlightenment, challenging the authority of a demiurge who seeks to keep humanity in ignorance.

Core Principles of Luciferianism

Luciferianism is built on several core principles that define its philosophy and practice. These principles are not merely abstract ideas; they are intended to be lived, experienced, and integrated into the life of the practitioner.

1. **Rebellion Against Conformity:**
   At the heart of Luciferianism is a deep-seated rebellion against conformity, dogma, and imposed limitations. Luciferianism celebrates the defiance of

societal norms and encourages individuals to question authority, think critically, and forge their own path. This rebellion is not an aimless defiance but a purposeful quest for personal sovereignty and self-determination.

2. **Self-Deification:**
One of the most distinctive aspects of Luciferianism is its focus on self-deification—the belief that each individual has the potential to become a god unto themselves. This is not a call for delusional grandeur but an invitation to realize the full potential of one's being through the pursuit of knowledge, self-mastery, and the integration of all aspects of the self, both light and dark.

3. **The Pursuit of Knowledge:**
Knowledge, particularly esoteric or forbidden knowledge, is highly valued in Luciferianism. The light of Lucifer is seen as the illumination that dispels ignorance and reveals the deeper truths of existence. Luciferianism encourages the seeker to explore all forms of knowledge, from the mundane to the mystical, and to use that knowledge as a tool for personal and spiritual empowerment.

4. **Embrace of Darkness:**
Unlike many spiritual paths that focus

solely on the light, Luciferianism embraces both light and darkness as essential components of the self and the cosmos. Darkness is not viewed as evil but as a necessary force for growth, transformation, and empowerment. The Luciferian path teaches that by confronting and integrating the shadow aspects of the self, one can achieve a more complete and powerful state of being.

5. **Individual Sovereignty:**
Luciferianism places a strong emphasis on the sovereignty of the individual. It teaches that each person has the power and responsibility to shape their own destiny, free from the constraints of external authority. This principle of individual sovereignty is closely linked to the concept of self-deification, as the Luciferian seeks to become the master of their own fate.

Lucifer as a Symbol of Enlightenment and Rebellion

Lucifer, as a symbol, represents the archetype of the enlightened rebel—the one who dares to challenge the established order in pursuit of higher knowledge and personal freedom. In this sense, Lucifer is not an adversary to humanity but a liberator who empowers individuals to rise above their limitations and claim their own divinity.

The image of Lucifer as the light-bringer is central to this philosophy. Just as the morning star heralds the dawn, Lucifer illuminates the path to enlightenment, guiding the seeker through the darkness of ignorance and into the light of wisdom. This illumination is not merely intellectual but is a deeply transformative process that involves the integration of the self in all its aspects—light and dark, conscious and unconscious, divine and demonic.

However, this path is not without its challenges. The journey of the Luciferian is one of self-discovery, transformation, and often, confrontation with the shadow aspects of the self. The shadow, as described by Carl Jung, represents the unconscious and often repressed aspects of the personality. In Luciferianism, the shadow is not something to be feared or suppressed but to be acknowledged, embraced, and integrated. This process of integration is seen as essential to achieving true enlightenment and self-deification.

Lucifer, as the archetypal rebel, also represents the spirit of resistance against tyranny, whether that tyranny is external (in the form of oppressive authority) or internal (in the form of limiting beliefs and fears). The Luciferian path teaches that true freedom can only be attained by confronting and overcoming these forms of tyranny, both within and without.

Conclusion: The Luciferian Path in the Modern World

In the modern world, Luciferianism continues to attract those who seek a path of individual empowerment, self-discovery, and spiritual enlightenment. It offers a way to transcend the limitations imposed by society, religion, and even the self, leading to a state of personal sovereignty and divine realization.

As a spiritual path, Luciferianism is deeply relevant in an age where conformity, dogma, and the suppression of individuality are still prevalent. It speaks to those who yearn for freedom, who seek to challenge the status quo, and who are willing to explore the depths of their own being in the quest for enlightenment.

As we proceed to explore the intersections between Luciferianism and Aghora, it is important to keep these core principles in mind. Both traditions, though culturally distinct, share a common goal: the pursuit of enlightenment through the embrace of darkness, the breaking of taboos, and the transcendence of conventional morality. In the next chapter, we will turn our attention to the Aghora tradition, delving into its practices, philosophies, and the unique ways in which it mirrors the Luciferian path.

CHAPTER 2: THE PATH OF AGHORA

Aghora, one of the most radical and misunderstood paths within Tantric Hinduism, is a tradition that delves into the darkest and most taboo aspects of existence to achieve spiritual liberation. Aghoris, the practitioners of this path, are often seen as enigmatic figures, shrouded in mystery and fear. They challenge societal norms and religious orthodoxy by engaging in practices that are considered abhorrent by conventional standards—meditating in cremation grounds, using human skulls as ritual vessels, and embracing filth and impurity. Yet, beneath these shocking practices lies a profound spiritual philosophy that seeks to transcend duality, achieve unity with the divine, and confront the ultimate realities of life and death.

Historical Background of Aghora

The Aghora tradition is rooted in the broader framework of Tantra, a spiritual system that emphasizes the use of rituals, symbols, and physical practices to achieve spiritual liberation. Tantra itself is a complex and multifaceted tradition, with numerous schools and interpretations, ranging from the purely philosophical to the intensely ritualistic. Aghora represents one of the most extreme manifestations of Tantric practice, focusing on the direct confrontation with death, impurity, and the shadow aspects of existence.

The origins of Aghora can be traced back to the medieval period in India, where it emerged as a distinct tradition within the larger Tantric movement. The word "Aghora" is derived from the Sanskrit term "Aghora," which means "not terrifying" or "beyond fear." This name reflects the Aghori's aspiration to transcend all fears, including the fear of death, impurity, and the unknown. The Aghoris believe that by confronting and embracing what society deems as terrifying or impure, they can achieve a state of non-duality, where all distinctions between sacred and profane, pure and impure, are dissolved.

Aghora is closely associated with the worship of the goddess Kali, a fierce and powerful deity who embodies both creation and destruction. Kali is often depicted as a dark-skinned goddess with a garland of skulls, standing on the body of her consort, Shiva. She represents the raw, untamed energy of the universe, the force of time and change that devours everything in its path. For the Aghoris, Kali is both mother and destroyer, a deity who must be worshipped and appeased through acts of extreme devotion and surrender.

The Aghori path is not for the faint of heart. It requires a willingness to engage with the most abject and terrifying aspects of existence, to see the divine in the midst of death and decay, and to embrace the totality of life without judgment or aversion. The Aghori's practices are designed to break down the barriers of fear, disgust, and attachment, leading to a state of spiritual liberation known as moksha.

The Life and Teachings of Notable Aghori Practitioners

Throughout history, there have been several notable Aghori practitioners who have left a lasting impact on the tradition. One of the most famous Aghoris was Baba Kinaram, a 17th-century ascetic who is considered the founding figure of the modern Aghora tradition. Baba Kinaram is said to have lived for over 150 years, spending much of his time in meditation and austerities in the cremation grounds of Varanasi, one of the holiest cities in India.

According to legend, Baba Kinaram was initiated into the Aghora path by Dattatreya, a deity who is revered as an incarnation of the Hindu trinity—Brahma, Vishnu, and Shiva. Dattatreya is often depicted as a wandering ascetic with three heads, symbolizing his mastery over creation, preservation, and destruction. Under Dattatreya's guidance, Baba Kinaram is said to have attained a state of spiritual enlightenment, becoming a powerful healer and guru.

Baba Kinaram's teachings emphasized the importance of seeing the divine in all things, regardless of their outward appearance. He taught that the distinctions between pure and impure, sacred and profane, are ultimately illusions that must be transcended in order to achieve spiritual liberation. Baba Kinaram established the Kinaram Ashram in Varanasi, which remains a center for Aghori practices to this day.

Another influential figure in the Aghora tradition was Aghori Vimalananda, a 20th-century practitioner whose life and teachings were chronicled by Robert E. Svoboda in the *Aghora* trilogy. Vimalananda was known for his intense devotion to Kali and his mastery of various Tantric practices, including the use of mantras, yantras, and rituals involving cremation grounds. Vimalananda's teachings, as recorded by Svoboda, offer a rare glimpse into the inner workings of the Aghori path, revealing both its spiritual depths and its potential dangers.

Vimalananda emphasized the importance of direct experience in spiritual practice, urging his students to go beyond intellectual understanding and to confront the raw realities of life and death. He believed that true spiritual growth could only be achieved by facing one's fears head-on, whether through meditating in a cremation ground, performing rituals with human remains, or engaging in other practices that challenge the ego and break down the barriers of conventional morality.

Core Beliefs and Practices of Aghora

The Aghora tradition is characterized by several core beliefs and practices that set it apart from other spiritual paths. These practices are designed to lead the practitioner to a state of non-duality, where all distinctions between self and other, sacred and profane, life and death, are dissolved.

1. **Confrontation with Death:**
   One of the most distinctive aspects of Aghora is its focus on the direct confrontation with death. Aghoris believe that by meditating in cremation grounds, handling human remains, and engaging in rituals that involve death and decay, they can transcend the fear of death and achieve spiritual liberation. The cremation ground, known as a "smashan" in Sanskrit,

is considered a sacred space where the veil between life and death is thin, allowing the practitioner to commune with the divine and confront the ultimate reality of impermanence.

2. **Embrace of Impurity:**
Aghoris deliberately seek out what is considered impure or taboo by society, believing that by embracing impurity, they can transcend duality and achieve a state of non-duality. This includes practices such as smearing their bodies with the ashes of the dead, consuming alcohol and meat (which are typically avoided by orthodox Hindus), and using human skulls as ritual vessels. For the Aghori, these acts of transgression are not seen as defilement, but as a way of breaking down the ego and achieving union with the divine.

3. **Devotion to Kali:**
Kali, the fierce and powerful goddess of time and destruction, is the primary deity worshipped by Aghoris. Kali represents the raw, untamed energy of the universe, and her worship involves acts of extreme devotion and surrender. Aghoris believe that by surrendering to Kali, they can overcome the illusions of the ego and attain spiritual liberation. Kali is often

depicted in Aghori rituals as a terrifying yet compassionate mother who guides the practitioner through the darkness of the unknown and into the light of wisdom.

4. **Transcendence of Duality:**

A central tenet of Aghora is the belief that all distinctions between sacred and profane, pure and impure, life and death, are ultimately illusory. Aghoris seek to transcend these dualities by embracing the totality of existence, including its darkest and most abject aspects. This is reflected in their rituals, which often involve confronting and integrating the shadow aspects of the self. By doing so, the Aghori aims to achieve a state of non-duality, where all opposites are reconciled and the true nature of reality is revealed.

5. **Spiritual Alchemy:**

The practices of Aghora can be seen as a form of spiritual alchemy, where the base elements of existence—death, impurity, fear—are transformed into spiritual gold. This alchemical process is not merely symbolic, but is experienced directly through the rituals and practices of the Aghori. The goal of this alchemy is to achieve moksha, or spiritual liberation, where the individual soul is freed from the cycle of birth and death and merges with the divine.

The Symbolism of Kali and Other Deities in Aghora

Kali is the central deity in the Aghora tradition, and her symbolism is rich with meaning. As the goddess of time, destruction, and transformation, Kali embodies the raw, untamed energy of the universe. She is often depicted with a garland of skulls, a skirt of severed arms, and a blood-red tongue protruding from her mouth. Her appearance is both terrifying and awe-inspiring, reflecting her dual nature as both creator and destroyer.

For the Aghori, Kali is not merely a symbol, but a living presence who must be worshipped and appeased through acts of devotion and surrender. Kali represents the cosmic force of time and change, which devours everything in its path. Yet, she is also a compassionate mother who guides her devotees through the darkness of the unknown and into the light of wisdom.

In addition to Kali, Aghoris also revere Shiva, the lord of destruction and transformation. Shiva is often depicted as a wild ascetic who resides in cremation grounds, smeared with ashes and adorned with snakes. He represents the dissolution of the ego and the destruction of all illusions. Shiva is also associated with the cremation ground, where the cycle of birth and death is transcended.

Other deities worshipped by Aghoris include Bhairava, a fierce manifestation of Shiva who is often depicted with a trident and a skull, and Dattatreya, the ascetic deity who is considered the guru of the Aghora tradition. These deities represent different aspects of the divine, all of which are seen as manifestations of the same ultimate reality.

The Aghori Perspective on Life, Death, and Spiritual Liberation

The Aghori perspective on life and death is radically different from that of mainstream Hinduism. For the Aghori, death is not something to be feared or avoided, but is seen as an integral part of the spiritual journey. The cremation ground, where the dead are reduced to ashes, is considered a sacred space where the veil between life and death is thin, allowing the practitioner to commune with the divine and confront the ultimate reality of impermanence.

Aghoris believe that by confronting death directly —by meditating in cremation grounds, handling human remains, and engaging in rituals that involve death and decay—they can transcend the fear of death and achieve spiritual liberation. This liberation, known as moksha, is the ultimate goal of the Aghori path. Moksha represents the dissolution of the ego and the union of the individual soul with the divine, where all distinctions between self and other, life and death, are dissolved.

In the Aghori tradition, life and death are seen as two sides of the same coin. Both are part of the same cosmic process, and both must be embraced in order to achieve spiritual liberation. The Aghori does not see death as an end, but as a transition, a gateway to a higher state of consciousness. By confronting and embracing death, the Aghori seeks to transcend the cycle of birth and death and achieve union with the divine.

Conclusion: The Aghora Path in the Modern World

The Aghora tradition, with its radical practices and transgressive philosophy, may seem alien and even terrifying to the modern mind. Yet, it offers profound insights into the nature of existence and the path to spiritual liberation. In a world that often shuns death, impurity, and the shadow aspects of life, the Aghori path challenges us to confront these realities head-on, to see the divine in all things, and to transcend the dualities that bind us.

As we proceed to explore the intersections between Aghora and Luciferianism, it is important to keep these core principles in mind. Both traditions, though culturally distinct, share a common goal:

the pursuit of enlightenment through the embrace of darkness, the breaking of taboos, and the transcendence of conventional morality. In the next chapter, we will delve into how these two paths, despite their differences, converge in their approach to spiritual alchemy and the transformative power of the left-hand path.

CHAPTER 3: DARKNESS AS DIVINITY

As we continue our journey into the convergence of Aghora and Luciferianism, we arrive at a concept that is central to both traditions: the embrace of darkness as a path to divinity. In many spiritual systems, darkness is often equated with evil, ignorance, and fear. However, within the frameworks of Aghora and Luciferianism, darkness is not something to be feared or avoided; rather, it is an essential aspect of the divine, a source of power, transformation, and ultimately, enlightenment.

The Concept of Darkness in Spiritual Traditions

Darkness has been a powerful symbol in spiritual traditions across the world, often representing the unknown, the mysterious, and the terrifying. In many cultures, darkness is associated with death, the underworld, and forces that are perceived as malevolent or chaotic. This association is not without reason; darkness obscures, confounds, and can evoke deep-seated fears within the human psyche.

In Western religious traditions, darkness is frequently depicted as the antithesis of light. In Christianity, for example, darkness is often used as a metaphor for sin, evil, and separation from God. The imagery of the "Prince of Darkness" as a representation of Satan reinforces the idea that darkness is something to be overcome, something that stands in opposition to divine light and goodness.

However, this dualistic view of light as good and darkness as evil is not universal. In many esoteric traditions, as well as in the paths of Aghora and Luciferianism, darkness is seen not as a force to be vanquished but as a vital component of the spiritual journey. Darkness is recognized as the womb of creation, the fertile ground from which all life emerges. It is within the darkness that transformation occurs, where the old is destroyed to make way for the new, and where the seeker can confront the deepest aspects of their soul.

Lucifer: The Light-Bringer in the Darkness

Lucifer, whose name means "light-bringer" or "morning star," embodies the paradox of light emerging from darkness. In Luciferianism, Lucifer is not merely a symbol of rebellion against divine authority, but also a representation of the light that shines through the dark, illuminating hidden truths and offering the seeker a path to enlightenment.

The mythological figure of Lucifer has long been associated with the concept of darkness. In Christian tradition, Lucifer is often depicted as the fallen angel who, through his pride and defiance, was cast out of heaven into the abyss of hell—a place of eternal darkness. However, Luciferianism reinterprets this myth, viewing Lucifer's fall not as a condemnation, but as an act of liberation. Lucifer's descent into darkness is seen as a journey into the depths of the self, a necessary step in the pursuit of knowledge and self-realization.

In this context, Lucifer represents the light of consciousness that pierces through the darkness of ignorance and fear. The darkness that surrounds Lucifer is not an evil to be vanquished, but a necessary condition for the emergence of enlightenment. The light that Lucifer brings is not the blinding, all-encompassing light of divine omnipotence, but a subtle, guiding flame that reveals the hidden and the obscure, encouraging the seeker to explore the unknown.

Lucifer's association with the morning star—the

first light that appears in the pre-dawn sky—further reinforces this idea. The morning star is a beacon of hope, a promise of the coming day, yet it shines most brightly in the darkness of night. This symbolism reflects the Luciferian belief that true enlightenment can only be achieved by confronting and integrating the dark aspects of existence.

Kali: The Dark Mother of Creation and Destruction

In the Aghora tradition, the goddess Kali embodies the divine power of darkness in a way that is both terrifying and awe-inspiring. Kali is a complex and multifaceted deity, representing the forces of time, change, destruction, and creation. She is often depicted with dark skin, wild hair, and a garland of skulls, holding a severed head in one of her hands and a bloodied sword in another. Her fearsome appearance is a stark reminder of the impermanence of life and the inevitability of death.

For the Aghori, Kali is the ultimate embodiment of the divine feminine, the dark mother who gives birth to the universe and destroys it in her cosmic dance. She is both nurturer and destroyer, creator and annihilator. In her dark form, Kali represents the primal forces of the universe that are beyond human comprehension, forces that can only be approached through surrender and devotion.

Kali's association with the cremation ground—a place of death, decay, and transformation—underscores her role as the goddess who governs the cycle of life and death. The cremation ground is where the Aghori performs their rituals, confronting death directly and seeking to transcend the fear of mortality. In the presence of Kali, the Aghori is reminded that all things are temporary, and that true liberation can only be attained by embracing the impermanence of existence.

Kali's darkness is not a void, but a fertile ground for spiritual growth. It is in the darkness of Kali's womb that the seed of enlightenment is planted, nurtured by the forces of destruction and creation. The Aghori seeks to merge with Kali, to become one with her cosmic dance, and in doing so, to transcend the dualities of life and death, light and dark.

The Philosophical Implications of Embracing Darkness

The embrace of darkness in both Luciferianism and Aghora has profound philosophical implications. In these traditions, darkness is not merely the absence of light, but a positive force in its own right—a force that is essential for the process of transformation and spiritual growth.

One of the key philosophical tenets of both traditions is the rejection of dualism—the idea that the world is divided into opposing forces of good and evil, light and dark. Instead, Luciferianism and Aghora propose a non-dualistic view of reality, where light and darkness are seen as complementary aspects of the same underlying truth. In this view, darkness is not something to be feared or eradicated, but embraced as a necessary part of the spiritual journey.

In Luciferianism, this non-dualistic approach is reflected in the concept of the "light-bringer" who emerges from darkness. The Luciferian path teaches that true enlightenment can only be achieved by integrating both the light and dark aspects of the self. This integration involves confronting the shadow—the unconscious, repressed parts of the psyche—and bringing it into the light of awareness. By doing so, the seeker attains a more complete and balanced understanding of themselves and the world.

In Aghora, the non-dualistic philosophy is embodied in the worship of Kali, who represents both the creative and destructive forces of the universe. The Aghori seeks to transcend the dualities of life and death, purity and impurity, by embracing the totality of existence. This transcendence is achieved through rituals and practices that confront the darkness directly, dissolving the ego and revealing the underlying unity of all things.

Both traditions challenge the conventional moral dichotomies of good versus evil, light versus dark. They propose that true spiritual liberation can only be attained by moving beyond these simplistic binaries and embracing the full spectrum of existence. In this way, darkness becomes not a hindrance to spiritual growth, but a catalyst for transformation.

The Transformative Power of Facing and Integrating the Shadow

The concept of the shadow, as developed by the psychologist Carl Jung, is central to understanding the transformative power of darkness in both Luciferianism and Aghora. The shadow represents the unconscious aspects of the psyche—those parts of the self that are repressed, denied, or feared. In Jungian psychology, the process of individuation—the journey towards self-realization and wholeness—involves confronting and integrating the shadow.

In Luciferianism, the shadow is seen as a source of untapped power and potential. By confronting the shadow, the Luciferian seeks to reclaim those parts of themselves that have been denied or repressed. This confrontation is not easy; it requires the courage to face one's deepest fears, desires, and weaknesses. However, by bringing the shadow into the light of consciousness, the Luciferian is able to integrate these aspects of the self, achieving a more complete and empowered state of being.

The rituals and practices of Luciferianism often involve symbolic acts of shadow integration. These may include meditations on the darker aspects of the self, invocations of Lucifer as the light-bringer who illuminates the shadow, and rituals that challenge the practitioner to confront their fears and limitations. Through these practices, the Luciferian seeks to achieve a state of self-deification, where the boundaries between light and dark, divine and demonic, are transcended.

In Aghora, the process of shadow integration is taken to an even more radical extreme. The Aghori deliberately seeks out what is considered impure, taboo, or terrifying by society, confronting the shadow aspects of existence in their most visceral form. This may include meditating in cremation grounds, handling human remains, or engaging in rituals that involve confronting death and decay. For the Aghori, these practices are not merely symbolic; they are direct, lived experiences of the shadow that challenge the ego and dissolve the barriers between self and other, life and death.

The transformative power of these practices lies

in their ability to dissolve the ego—the sense of a separate, individual self that is bound by fear, attachment, and dualistic thinking. By confronting the shadow and embracing the darkness, the Aghori and the Luciferian alike seek to transcend the limitations of the ego and achieve a state of non-duality, where all opposites are reconciled and the true nature of reality is revealed.

Conclusion: Darkness as a Path to Enlightenment

In both Luciferianism and Aghora, darkness is not merely a backdrop against which the drama of life unfolds; it is an active, dynamic force that drives the process of spiritual transformation. The embrace of darkness is seen as essential for the journey towards enlightenment, as it allows the seeker to confront and integrate the shadow aspects of the self, dissolve the ego, and achieve a state of non-duality.

This approach to spirituality challenges the conventional wisdom that equates light with good and darkness with evil. Instead, it proposes a more nuanced understanding of the divine, one that recognizes the necessity of both light and dark, creation and destruction, in the process of spiritual evolution. In this way, darkness becomes a path to divinity, a source of power and wisdom that, when embraced, leads to the ultimate goal of spiritual liberation.

As we move forward in this exploration of the convergence between Luciferianism and Aghora, we will delve deeper into the rituals and practices that embody this embrace of darkness. In the next chapter, we will examine the rituals of the left-hand path, exploring how these practices serve as vehicles for transformation, empowerment, and the realization of the divine within.

CHAPTER 4: RITUALS OF THE LEFT-HAND PATH

Rituals are a crucial component of any spiritual practice, serving as the bridge between the material and the divine, the physical and the metaphysical. In the left-hand path, rituals take on a particularly potent role, as they are designed to confront and transcend conventional morality, societal norms, and the limitations of the ego. Both Luciferianism and Aghora emphasize the importance of ritual as a means of achieving spiritual transformation, self-deification, and direct communion with the divine.

In this chapter, we will explore the rituals that define the left-hand path in both Luciferianism and Aghora. These rituals are not for the faint of heart; they demand a willingness to confront fear, darkness, and the shadow aspects of existence. Yet, through these rituals, practitioners seek to attain profound spiritual empowerment, enlightenment, and a deeper understanding of the mysteries of life and death.

The Purpose and Power of Ritual in the Left-Hand Path

Rituals in the left-hand path serve multiple purposes. They are tools for self-transformation, methods for invoking and interacting with divine or supernatural forces, and vehicles for exploring the depths of the psyche. Unlike the rituals of the right-hand path, which often focus on purity, harmony, and alignment with a higher moral order, the rituals of the left-hand path challenge the practitioner to engage with the darker, more chaotic aspects of existence.

One of the primary purposes of ritual in the left-hand path is to break down the boundaries of the ego. The ego, with its attachments, fears, and limitations, is seen as an obstacle to spiritual enlightenment. Through ritual, the practitioner seeks to transcend the ego, dissolving the illusion of separateness and achieving a state of non-duality. This is accomplished by confronting the shadow, embracing darkness, and engaging in acts that challenge societal taboos and personal fears.

In Luciferianism, rituals often involve invocations of Lucifer as the light-bringer and the adversary. These rituals are designed to empower the practitioner, to awaken the divine spark within, and to facilitate the process of self-deification. In Aghora, rituals are focused on the worship of Kali and the direct confrontation with death and impurity. The Aghori seeks to merge with the divine through acts of transgression, surrender, and the dissolution of dualities.

The power of these rituals lies in their ability to transform the practitioner on a deep, fundamental level. By engaging with the forces of darkness and chaos, the practitioner is able to tap into a wellspring of spiritual power, wisdom, and insight that is otherwise inaccessible. These rituals are not merely symbolic; they are direct, lived experiences that alter the practitioner's consciousness and bring them closer to the divine.

Luciferian Rituals: Invoking the Light-Bringer

Luciferian rituals are designed to invoke the presence of Lucifer as a guiding force in the practitioner's life. These rituals often involve acts of rebellion, self-empowerment, and the conscious integration of both light and dark aspects of the self. The goal of these rituals is to achieve self-deification—a state in which the practitioner becomes a god unto themselves, fully in control of their destiny and in possession of profound spiritual insight.

One common form of Luciferian ritual is the invocation of Lucifer as the light-bringer. This ritual may begin with the practitioner entering a meditative state, focusing their mind on the qualities of Lucifer—enlightenment, rebellion, and self-sovereignty. The practitioner may then recite invocations or prayers that call upon Lucifer to illuminate their path, to guide them through the darkness of ignorance and fear, and to empower them in their quest for knowledge and self-realization.

The ritual may also involve the use of symbols and tools associated with Luciferianism. These could include the pentagram (a symbol of protection and the balance of elements), the black flame (representing the inner divine spark), and the serpent (a symbol of wisdom and transformation). The practitioner may create an altar dedicated to Lucifer, placing these symbols upon it and lighting candles or incense to create an atmosphere of sacredness and focus.

As the ritual progresses, the practitioner may engage in acts that symbolize their rejection of conventional morality and their embrace of the left-hand path. This could involve reciting oaths of self-sovereignty, performing symbolic acts of rebellion, or meditating on the concept of self-deification. The ritual may culminate in a moment of communion with Lucifer, where the practitioner feels a deep connection with the divine and experiences a profound sense of empowerment and clarity.

Another key aspect of Luciferian ritual is the integration of the shadow. This involves confronting the darker aspects of the self—those parts of the psyche that are repressed, feared, or denied. The practitioner may engage in shadow work, which could include journaling, meditative visualization, or role-playing exercises that bring the shadow into consciousness. By acknowledging and integrating these shadow aspects, the practitioner is able to achieve a more complete and powerful state of being.

Luciferian rituals often emphasize personal freedom and the rejection of external authority. The practitioner is encouraged to question dogma, to think critically, and to forge their own path. This spirit of rebellion is central to the Luciferian ethos, which views the pursuit of knowledge and self-empowerment as the highest goals of spiritual practice.

Aghori Rituals: Confronting Death and Impurity

Aghori rituals are among the most extreme and challenging in the world of spiritual practice. These rituals are designed to confront the practitioner with the realities of death, impurity, and the shadow aspects of existence. Through these confrontations, the Aghori seeks to transcend fear, dissolve the ego, and achieve a state of non-duality where all distinctions between sacred and profane, pure and impure, are obliterated.

One of the most iconic and misunderstood Aghori rituals is the meditation in cremation grounds. The cremation ground, or smashan, is a place where the bodies of the dead are burned, and it is considered one of the most sacred and powerful places for an Aghori. By meditating in such a place, surrounded by death and decay, the Aghori confronts the impermanence of life and the inevitability of death. This practice is not merely an intellectual exercise; it is a direct, visceral encounter with mortality, designed to strip away the illusions of the ego and reveal the underlying reality of existence.

The Aghori may also engage in rituals that involve the use of human remains, such as skulls or ashes. These objects are not seen as macabre or grotesque, but as sacred tools that connect the practitioner with the cycle of life and death. Aghoris may use skulls as drinking vessels, or they may smear their bodies with ashes from the cremation grounds as a symbol of their acceptance of death and their rejection of the distinctions between pure and impure.

In addition to their practices involving death, Aghoris are known for their deliberate embrace of impurity. This can include the consumption of substances that are considered taboo or unclean by conventional standards, such as alcohol, meat, or even human flesh. These acts of transgression are not performed out of hedonism or perversity, but as a means of challenging and dissolving the ego. By embracing what is considered impure, the Aghori seeks to transcend duality and achieve a state of non-duality where all things are seen as equal expressions of the divine.

Another important aspect of Aghori ritual is the worship of Kali, the dark mother who embodies both creation and destruction. Aghori rituals dedicated to Kali often involve acts of extreme devotion and surrender. The practitioner may offer blood sacrifices, chant mantras, or perform elaborate rituals designed to invoke Kali's presence. These rituals are not for the faint-hearted; they demand a willingness to face the darkest aspects of existence and to surrender completely to the will of the goddess.

The ultimate goal of Aghori rituals is to achieve moksha, or spiritual liberation. This is accomplished through the dissolution of the ego, the transcendence of duality, and the realization of non-duality, where the practitioner experiences themselves as one with the divine. The Aghori path is a radical and challenging journey, but for those who are called to it, it offers the promise of profound spiritual transformation and liberation.

The Role of Ritual in Self-Transformation and Spiritual Empowerment

In both Luciferianism and Aghora, rituals serve as powerful tools for self-transformation and spiritual empowerment. These rituals are not merely symbolic; they are direct, lived experiences that engage the practitioner on multiple levels —physical, emotional, mental, and spiritual. Through ritual, the practitioner is able to access deeper layers of consciousness, confront their fears and limitations, and tap into the transformative power of the divine.

One of the key functions of ritual in the left-hand path is to dissolve the boundaries of the ego. The ego, with its attachments, fears, and dualistic thinking, is seen as an obstacle to spiritual enlightenment. By engaging in rituals that challenge and transcend the ego, the practitioner is able to achieve a state of non-duality, where all distinctions between self and other, light and dark, sacred and profane, are dissolved.

Another important function of ritual is the invocation of divine or supernatural forces. In Luciferianism, this often involves invoking the presence of Lucifer as a guiding force in the practitioner's life. In Aghora, it may involve invoking the presence of Kali or other deities associated with death, destruction, and transformation. These invocations are not merely acts of worship; they are ways of establishing a direct connection with the divine, allowing the practitioner to draw upon the power, wisdom, and insight of these forces.

Rituals in the left-hand path also serve as vehicles for exploring the depths of the psyche. By confronting the shadow and integrating the darker aspects of the self, the practitioner is able to achieve a more complete and powerful state of being. This process of shadow integration is essential for achieving self-deification in Luciferianism and moksha in Aghora. It is through ritual that the practitioner is able to confront their fears, dissolve their attachments, and realize their true nature as divine beings.

Finally, rituals in the left-hand path are acts of rebellion and transgression. They challenge societal norms, conventional morality, and the limitations of the ego. By engaging in these acts of rebellion, the practitioner asserts their sovereignty and freedom, declaring themselves as masters of their own destiny. This spirit of rebellion is central to the Luciferian ethos, which views the pursuit of knowledge and self-empowerment as the highest goals of spiritual practice.

Conclusion: The Transformative Power of Ritual

Rituals in the left-hand path are powerful tools

for self-transformation, spiritual empowerment, and the realization of the divine within. Whether through the invocation of Lucifer as the light-bringer, the meditation in cremation grounds, or the embrace of impurity, these rituals challenge the practitioner to confront their fears, dissolve their ego, and achieve a state of non-duality.

The transformative power of these rituals lies in their ability to engage the practitioner on multiple levels—physical, emotional, mental, and spiritual. They are not merely symbolic acts, but direct, lived experiences that alter the practitioner's consciousness and bring them closer to the divine. Through these rituals, the practitioner is able to access deeper layers of consciousness, confront the shadow aspects of the self, and tap into the transformative power of the divine.

As we continue our exploration of the convergence between Luciferianism and Aghora, we will delve into the specific symbols, tools, and practices that embody the embrace of darkness in both traditions. In the next chapter, we will examine the symbolic significance of the graveyard and the fire, exploring how these elements play a crucial role in the rituals and spiritual practices of the left-hand path.

CHAPTER 5: THE GRAVEYARD AND THE FIRE

The symbols of the graveyard and the fire hold profound significance in both Luciferianism and Aghora, representing the dual forces of destruction and transformation. These elements are not merely metaphorical; they are deeply embedded in the rituals and practices of both traditions, serving as powerful tools for confronting death, purifying the soul, and achieving spiritual rebirth. In this chapter, we will explore the symbolic and literal importance of the graveyard and the fire in these paths, and how they facilitate the journey toward enlightenment.

The Graveyard: A Place of Death and Transformation

In many cultures, the graveyard is seen as a place of fear, a realm where the dead rest and where the living rarely venture. However, in both Luciferianism and Aghora, the graveyard is revered as a sacred space, a liminal zone where the veil between life and death is thin, and where profound spiritual insights can be gained.

For the Aghori, the graveyard—or *smashan*—is the most sacred of all spaces. It is here, amidst the ashes of the dead, that the Aghori performs their most intense spiritual practices. The graveyard is not merely a resting place for the dead; it is a powerful site of transformation, where the practitioner confronts the impermanence of life and the inevitability of death. The Aghori believes that by meditating in the graveyard, they can transcend the fear of death and dissolve the illusions of the ego.

The symbolism of the graveyard in Aghora is multifaceted. It represents the cycle of life, death, and rebirth, and the ever-present reality of impermanence. The cremation ground is a place where the physical body is reduced to ashes, symbolizing the dissolution of the ego and the return to the formless essence of the divine. For the Aghori, the graveyard is not a place of sorrow or despair; it is a place of liberation, where the soul is freed from the bondage of the physical body and the cycle of birth and death.

Aghori rituals in the graveyard often involve

meditating on death, chanting mantras, and using human remains in their practices. These acts are not meant to be morbid or grotesque; rather, they are seen as powerful tools for spiritual purification and transformation. By confronting death directly, the Aghori seeks to overcome the fear of mortality and to realize the eternal nature of the soul.

In Luciferianism, the graveyard also holds significant symbolic meaning. While the physical practice of meditating in graveyards may not be as central as it is in Aghora, the symbolism of the graveyard as a place of death, decay, and transformation is deeply embedded in Luciferian thought. The graveyard represents the finality of death, the dissolution of the physical form, and the return to the earth. It is a reminder of the impermanence of all things and the necessity of embracing death as a natural part of the spiritual journey.

For the Luciferian, the graveyard symbolizes the confrontation with the shadow—the dark, repressed aspects of the self that must be acknowledged and integrated for true spiritual growth. Just as the body decays and returns to the earth, so too must the ego dissolve and return to the formless essence of the divine. This process of dissolution and transformation is central to the Luciferian path, where the practitioner seeks to achieve self-deification by embracing both the light and dark aspects of existence.

The Fire: Purification and Renewal

Fire is a universal symbol of purification, transformation, and renewal, and it holds a central place in the rituals of both Aghora and Luciferianism. Fire is seen as a powerful, cleansing force that can burn away impurities, destroy the old, and make way for the new. In both traditions, fire is not merely a physical element; it is a symbol of the divine energy that drives the process of spiritual transformation.

In Aghora, fire is intimately connected with the cremation ground, where the bodies of the dead are burned to ashes. The cremation fire is a powerful symbol of purification, representing the destruction of the physical form and the release of the soul from the cycle of birth and death. The Aghori sees the fire as a manifestation of the goddess Kali, the force of destruction and creation, who devours all things in her cosmic dance.

The ritual use of fire in Aghora extends beyond the cremation ground. Aghoris may perform fire rituals, known as *homa* or *havan*, where offerings are made into the sacred fire. These rituals are seen as acts of devotion and surrender, where the practitioner offers their desires, attachments, and ego to the fire, symbolizing their willingness to be purified and transformed by the divine. The fire consumes these offerings, transforming them into smoke and ash, which rise to the heavens as a symbol of spiritual liberation.

Fire in Aghora is also associated with the inner fire, known as *kundalini*, the spiritual energy that lies dormant at the base of the spine. Through intense meditation and spiritual practice, the Aghori seeks to awaken this inner fire, which rises through the chakras, purifying the body and mind, and ultimately leading to the realization of non-duality and union with the divine.

In Luciferianism, fire is equally significant, symbolizing both the light of Lucifer and the transformative power of the divine. The black flame, a key symbol in Luciferian rituals, represents the inner divine spark—the aspect of the self that is divine, sovereign, and capable of self-deification. The black flame is not merely a source of light; it is a source of power, a force that burns away ignorance and fear, and reveals the hidden truths of existence.

Luciferian rituals often involve the use of candles, fires, or other sources of flame, which are used to focus the practitioner's mind and to symbolize the illumination of the path. The fire represents the light of Lucifer, the morning star, who guides the seeker through the darkness of ignorance and fear. By meditating on the flame, the practitioner seeks to connect with this inner light, to awaken their divine potential, and to achieve self-empowerment.

The fire in Luciferianism also represents the process of spiritual alchemy, where the base elements of the self—fears, desires, and attachments—are transformed into spiritual gold. Just as the alchemist uses fire to purify and transform metals, so too does the Luciferian use the fire of spiritual practice to purify the soul and to achieve self-deification.

The Cremation Ground: A Sacred Space of Transformation

The cremation ground, or *smashan*, is one of the most sacred spaces in the Aghora tradition. It is a place where the physical body is reduced to ashes, symbolizing the dissolution of the ego and the return to the formless essence of the divine. The cremation ground is a powerful symbol of impermanence, reminding the practitioner that all things are temporary and that true liberation can only be attained by transcending the physical form.

For the Aghori, the cremation ground is not a place of fear or despair; it is a place of profound spiritual transformation. By meditating in the cremation ground, surrounded by death and decay, the Aghori confronts the impermanence of life and the inevitability of death. This confrontation is not merely an intellectual exercise; it is a direct, visceral experience that strips away the illusions of the ego and reveals the underlying reality of existence.

The cremation ground is also a place of ritual power. The ashes of the dead, the smoke of the cremation fire, and the presence of death itself are seen as powerful tools for spiritual purification and transformation. The Aghori may use the ashes of the dead in their rituals, smearing them on their bodies as a symbol of their acceptance of death and their rejection of the distinctions between pure and impure. These rituals are not meant to be morbid or grotesque; they are acts of devotion and surrender, where the practitioner seeks to merge with the divine by embracing the totality of existence.

The cremation ground is also a place of intense spiritual energy. The Aghori believes that the presence of death and the dissolution of the physical form create a powerful energy field that can be harnessed for spiritual practice. By meditating in this space, the Aghori seeks to tap into this energy, to dissolve the ego, and to achieve a state of non-duality where all distinctions between self and other, life and death, are obliterated.

In Luciferianism, while the physical act of meditating in a cremation ground may not be a common practice, the symbolism of the cremation ground as a place of death, transformation, and spiritual power is deeply resonant. The Luciferian path emphasizes the importance of confronting death, acknowledging the impermanence of all things, and embracing the process of transformation that death represents. The graveyard or cremation ground symbolizes the finality of death and the necessity of embracing it as a natural part of the spiritual journey.

For the Luciferian, the graveyard or cremation ground is a reminder of the impermanence of the physical form and the importance of focusing on the eternal aspects of the self—the inner divine spark, the black flame—that transcends physical death. By meditating on the symbolism of the cremation ground, the Luciferian seeks to dissolve the ego, to integrate the shadow, and to achieve a state of self-deification where the soul is liberated from the cycle of birth and death.

The Symbolism of Fire in Rituals

Fire, as a symbol of purification and transformation, plays a central role in the rituals of both Aghora and Luciferianism. In these traditions, fire is seen as a divine force that can burn away impurities, destroy the old, and make way for the new. Fire is not merely a physical element; it is a symbol of the divine energy that drives the process of spiritual transformation.

In Aghora, fire is intimately connected with the cremation ground, where the bodies of the dead are burned to ashes. The cremation fire is a powerful symbol of purification, representing the destruction of the physical form and the release of the soul from the cycle of birth and death. The Aghori sees the fire as a manifestation of the goddess Kali, the force of destruction and creation, who devours all things in her cosmic dance.

Fire rituals in Aghora, such as *homa* or *havan*, involve offerings made into the sacred fire. These rituals are acts of devotion and surrender, where the practitioner offers their desires, attachments, and ego to the fire, symbolizing their willingness to be purified and transformed by the divine. The fire consumes these offerings, transforming them into smoke and ash, which rise to the heavens as a symbol of spiritual liberation.

In Luciferianism, fire is equally significant, symbolizing both the light of Lucifer and the transformative power of the divine. The black flame, a key symbol in Luciferian rituals, represents the inner divine spark—the aspect of the self that is divine, sovereign, and capable of self-deification. The black flame is not merely a source of light; it is a source of power, a force that burns away ignorance and fear, and reveals the hidden truths of existence.

Luciferian rituals often involve the use of candles, fires, or other sources of flame, which are used to focus the practitioner's mind and to symbolize the illumination of the path. The fire represents the light of Lucifer, the morning star, who guides the seeker through the darkness of ignorance and fear. By meditating on the flame, the practitioner seeks to connect with this inner light, to awaken their divine potential, and to achieve self-empowerment.

Conclusion: The Graveyard and the Fire as Catalysts for Transformation

The graveyard and the fire are not merely symbols in the left-hand path; they are powerful catalysts for spiritual transformation. In both Aghora and Luciferianism, these elements serve as reminders of the impermanence of life, the inevitability of death, and the necessity of embracing both in the pursuit of spiritual liberation.

For the Aghori, the graveyard is a sacred space where the realities of death and impermanence are confronted head-on. It is a place where the physical form is reduced to ashes, and the soul is liberated from the cycle of birth and death. The fire, both in the cremation ground and in ritual, is a symbol of purification, destruction, and renewal, representing the divine energy of Kali that devours all things in her cosmic dance.

In Luciferianism, the graveyard and the fire symbolize the confrontation with the shadow, the dissolution of the ego, and the process of spiritual alchemy. The practitioner uses these symbols to connect with the inner divine spark, to awaken their potential for self-deification, and to achieve enlightenment through the embrace of both light and dark aspects of existence.

As we continue our exploration of the convergence between Aghora and Luciferianism, we will delve deeper into the practices that embody these symbols, examining how they serve as vehicles for self-transformation, spiritual empowerment, and the realization of the divine within. In the next chapter, we will explore the sacred and the profane, examining how both traditions use elements that are considered taboo or impure as tools for spiritual elevation and the dissolution of duality.

CHAPTER 6: THE SACRED AND THE PROFANE

In both Luciferianism and Aghora, the boundaries between the sacred and the profane are deliberately blurred, challenging the conventional dichotomies that dominate most spiritual and religious traditions. These paths do not shy away from the taboo, the impure, or the forbidden; instead, they embrace these elements as integral parts of the spiritual journey. By transgressing societal norms and engaging with the profane, practitioners of Luciferianism and Aghora seek to dissolve dualities, confront the shadow, and achieve a state of spiritual liberation where all things are seen as expressions of the divine.

In this chapter, we will explore how both traditions use the profane as a tool for spiritual elevation, examining the philosophical underpinnings of this approach, the rituals that embody it, and the transformative potential it offers to those who walk the left-hand path.

The Philosophical Underpinnings of the Sacred and the Profane

The distinction between the sacred and the profane is a fundamental concept in many religious and spiritual traditions. The sacred is often associated with purity, divinity, and the transcendent, while the profane is linked to impurity, sin, and the mundane. This dualistic worldview is reflected in the rituals, practices, and moral codes of numerous religious systems, where the sacred is revered and the profane is avoided or condemned.

However, in both Luciferianism and Aghora, this dualistic distinction is not only questioned but actively subverted. These traditions propose a non-dualistic understanding of reality, where the sacred and the profane are not seen as opposites but as complementary aspects of the same underlying truth. In this view, all things—whether deemed sacred or profane by societal standards—are ultimately expressions of the divine.

The philosophical foundation for this approach can be found in the concept of non-duality, which is central to both traditions. Non-duality, or *advaita*, posits that the apparent distinctions between opposites—light and dark, good and evil, sacred and profane—are illusory. In reality, all things are interconnected, and all dualities are reconciled in the ultimate oneness of the divine.

In Luciferianism, this non-dualistic philosophy is reflected in the embrace of both light and dark as essential components of the self and the cosmos. The Luciferian path teaches that true spiritual enlightenment can only be achieved by integrating the shadow—the repressed, feared, or denied aspects of the self. This integration involves confronting the profane, embracing it as a part of the self, and transcending the dualistic thinking that separates the sacred from the profane.

Aghora takes this concept to its extreme, with practices that deliberately transgress societal norms and engage with what is considered impure or taboo. The Aghori believes that by embracing impurity and transgression, they can dissolve the ego, transcend duality, and achieve a state of non-duality where all things are seen as expressions of the divine. For the Aghori, nothing is inherently impure or profane; all things, even the most abject and terrifying, are manifestations of the divine mother Kali, who embodies both creation and destruction.

Transgressive Rituals in Aghora

The rituals of Aghora are among the most transgressive and challenging in the world of spiritual practice. These rituals are designed to confront the practitioner with the realities of death, impurity, and the shadow aspects of existence, challenging societal norms and the limitations of the ego.

One of the most iconic and controversial practices in Aghora is the use of human remains in rituals. Aghoris may meditate in cremation grounds, use human skulls as ritual vessels, or smear their bodies with the ashes of the dead. These acts are not meant to be morbid or grotesque; rather, they are seen as powerful tools for spiritual purification and transformation. By confronting death directly and engaging with what society deems impure, the Aghori seeks to transcend the fear of mortality, dissolve the ego, and achieve a state of non-duality.

Another key aspect of Aghori practice is the deliberate consumption of substances that are considered taboo or unclean by conventional standards. This can include alcohol, meat, or even human flesh, consumed as part of a ritual offering to the goddess Kali. These acts of transgression are not performed out of hedonism or perversity, but as a means of challenging and dissolving the ego. By embracing what is considered impure, the Aghori seeks to transcend duality and achieve a state of non-duality where all things are seen as equal expressions of the divine.

The worship of Kali is central to these transgressive

practices. Kali, the dark mother who embodies both creation and destruction, is worshipped through rituals that involve intense devotion, surrender, and the confrontation with death and impurity. The Aghori offers their fears, desires, and attachments to Kali, surrendering completely to her divine power. Through this act of surrender, the practitioner seeks to merge with Kali, to become one with her cosmic dance, and to transcend the dualities of life and death, sacred and profane.

The Embrace of the Profane in Luciferianism

While the rituals of Luciferianism may not be as outwardly transgressive as those of Aghora, the philosophy behind them is similarly focused on the integration of the profane as a means of achieving spiritual enlightenment. Luciferianism emphasizes the importance of confronting and embracing the shadow—the repressed, feared, or denied aspects of the self—in order to achieve self-deification and spiritual empowerment.

One of the ways this is expressed in Luciferian practice is through the use of symbols and rituals that challenge conventional morality and societal norms. The pentagram, a symbol often associated with witchcraft and the occult, is used in Luciferian rituals as a symbol of protection, balance, and the integration of opposites. The serpent, a symbol of wisdom and transformation, is also central to Luciferian symbolism, representing the awakening of the inner divine spark and the pursuit of hidden knowledge.

Luciferian rituals often involve the invocation of Lucifer as the light-bringer and the adversary. These rituals may include acts of rebellion, self-empowerment, and the conscious integration of both light and dark aspects of the self. The goal of these rituals is to achieve self-deification—a state in which the practitioner becomes a god unto themselves, fully in control of their destiny and in possession of profound spiritual insight.

The embrace of the profane in Luciferianism is also reflected in the concept of the black flame, a symbol of the inner divine spark that burns within each individual. The black flame represents the aspect of the self that is divine, sovereign, and capable of self-deification. By meditating on the black flame and invoking its power, the practitioner seeks to awaken their divine potential and to achieve enlightenment through the integration of both light and dark.

Luciferianism also challenges conventional morality by rejecting the idea of sin or evil as absolute concepts. Instead, it proposes a more nuanced understanding of morality, where actions are judged based on their alignment with the individual's true will and their potential for spiritual growth. This rejection of dualistic morality allows the Luciferian to embrace the profane as a valid and necessary aspect of the spiritual journey, rather than something to be avoided or condemned.

The Transformative Potential of Embracing the Profane

The embrace of the profane in both Luciferianism and Aghora is not merely an act of rebellion or transgression; it is a powerful tool for spiritual transformation. By engaging with what is considered taboo, impure, or forbidden, the practitioner confronts the shadow aspects of the self, dissolves the ego, and achieves a state of non-duality where all things are seen as expressions of the divine.

In Aghora, the confrontation with death, impurity, and the profane is seen as essential for achieving spiritual liberation. The Aghori believes that by embracing the abject and the terrifying, they can dissolve the ego and transcend the dualities of life and death, sacred and profane. This process of dissolution and transformation is central to the Aghori path, where the practitioner seeks to merge with the divine through acts of surrender, devotion, and transgression.

In Luciferianism, the embrace of the profane is seen as a means of achieving self-deification and spiritual empowerment. The Luciferian path teaches that true enlightenment can only be achieved by integrating both light and dark aspects of the self, confronting the shadow, and embracing the totality of existence. By rejecting conventional morality and embracing the profane, the Luciferian seeks to achieve a state of spiritual sovereignty where they are fully in control of their destiny and in possession of profound spiritual insight.

The transformative potential of embracing the profane lies in its ability to challenge and dissolve the ego, to confront the shadow, and to achieve a state of non-duality where all distinctions between sacred and profane, pure and impure, are obliterated. In this state of non-duality, the practitioner experiences themselves as one with the divine, where all things—whether deemed sacred or profane by societal standards—are recognized as equal expressions of the divine.

Conclusion: The Sacred and the Profane as Paths to Enlightenment

The distinction between the sacred and the profane is a fundamental concept in many religious and spiritual traditions, but in both Luciferianism and Aghora, this distinction is deliberately blurred, challenged, and ultimately transcended. These paths teach that true spiritual enlightenment can only be achieved by embracing the totality of existence—light and dark, sacred and profane, pure and impure—as expressions of the divine.

In Aghora, the deliberate transgression of societal norms and the embrace of impurity are seen as essential tools for spiritual liberation. The Aghori seeks to dissolve the ego, confront the shadow, and achieve a state of non-duality where all things are seen as expressions of the divine mother Kali, who embodies both creation and destruction.

In Luciferianism, the integration of the profane is central to the process of self-deification and spiritual empowerment. The Luciferian path teaches that true enlightenment can only be achieved by confronting and embracing the shadow, rejecting conventional morality, and awakening the inner divine spark represented by the black flame.

As we continue our exploration of the convergence between Aghora and Luciferianism, we will delve into the alchemical processes that underlie these practices, examining how the embrace of the profane serves as a catalyst for spiritual transformation and the realization of the divine within. In the next chapter, we will explore the alchemy of the soul, focusing on the transformative journey from darkness to light and the ultimate goal of spiritual enlightenment.

CHAPTER 7: THE ALCHEMY OF THE SOUL

Alchemy, in its most esoteric sense, is the process of transforming the base elements of the self—our fears, desires, and limitations—into the spiritual gold of enlightenment and self-realization. Both Luciferianism and Aghora engage in a form of spiritual alchemy, where the practitioner seeks to transmute the darkness within into light, the mundane into the divine, and the profane into the sacred. This chapter explores the alchemical processes inherent in both traditions, focusing on how the journey from darkness to light serves as a catalyst for profound spiritual transformation.

The Concept of Spiritual Alchemy

Alchemy is often associated with the ancient pursuit of turning lead into gold, but in its deeper, spiritual context, alchemy is the process of transmuting the base elements of the human soul into their highest, most refined state. This process involves the purification of the self, the integration of the shadow, and the realization of one's divine potential. In both Luciferianism and Aghora, spiritual alchemy is not just a metaphor but a lived experience, a transformative journey that leads to self-deification or spiritual liberation.

The stages of alchemy, traditionally referred to as *nigredo* (blackening), *albedo* (whitening), *citrinitas* (yellowing), and *rubedo* (reddening), correspond to the stages of spiritual transformation. These stages are mirrored in the practices and philosophies of both Luciferianism and Aghora, where the practitioner must first confront and integrate the darkness within before they can achieve the enlightenment and empowerment that comes with the final stages of the alchemical process.

In the *nigredo* stage, the practitioner confronts the shadow—the unconscious, repressed parts of the psyche that must be brought into the light of awareness. This stage is often associated with the experience of the dark night of the soul, where the individual undergoes a period of intense inner turmoil and purification. In Luciferianism, this stage may involve confronting the darker aspects of the self through rituals that invoke the presence of Lucifer as the light-bringer, who guides the practitioner through the darkness of ignorance and fear.

In Aghora, the *nigredo* stage is embodied in the practices that confront death and impurity, such as meditating in cremation grounds or using human remains in rituals. These practices force the Aghori to confront the impermanence of life and the reality of death, dissolving the ego and preparing the soul for the subsequent stages of alchemical transformation.

The *albedo* stage represents the purification of the soul, where the practitioner begins to integrate the insights gained during the *nigredo* stage and to cleanse the self of impurities. This stage is often associated with the awakening of spiritual insight, where the practitioner begins to see beyond the dualities of light and dark, sacred and profane, and to recognize the underlying unity of all things.

In Luciferianism, the *albedo* stage may involve the awakening of the black flame—the inner divine spark that represents the potential for self-deification. The practitioner may engage in rituals that focus on the illumination of the path, invoking the presence of Lucifer to guide them towards the light of knowledge and wisdom. This stage is marked by the realization that the darkness within is not something to be feared or rejected, but a necessary part of the spiritual journey.

In Aghora, the *albedo* stage is reflected in the

practices of surrender and devotion to Kali, the dark mother who embodies both creation and destruction. The Aghori offers their desires, attachments, and ego to Kali, symbolically purifying the self and preparing the soul for the final stages of spiritual transformation.

The *citrinitas* stage represents the dawning of spiritual enlightenment, where the practitioner begins to realize their divine potential and to embody the qualities of the divine within themselves. This stage is often associated with the integration of both light and dark aspects of the self, where the practitioner achieves a state of balance and harmony.

In Luciferianism, the *citrinitas* stage may involve the full realization of the self as a divine being, where the practitioner achieves self-deification and becomes a god unto themselves. This stage is marked by a profound sense of empowerment, where the individual is fully in control of their destiny and possesses a deep understanding of the mysteries of existence.

In Aghora, the *citrinitas* stage is reflected in the attainment of non-duality, where the practitioner transcends the distinctions between sacred and profane, pure and impure, life and death. The Aghori experiences themselves as one with the divine, fully realizing their unity with Kali and the cosmos.

The *rubedo* stage represents the completion of the alchemical process, where the practitioner fully embodies the divine within themselves and achieves spiritual enlightenment or liberation. This stage is often associated with the experience of spiritual rebirth, where the individual emerges from the darkness of the *nigredo* stage transformed and illuminated.

In Luciferianism, the *rubedo* stage may involve the final integration of the shadow, where the practitioner fully embraces both light and dark as aspects of the self and achieves a state of spiritual sovereignty. This stage is marked by a profound sense of inner peace and fulfillment, where the individual is fully aligned with their true will and their divine potential.

In Aghora, the *rubedo* stage is reflected in the attainment of moksha, or spiritual liberation, where the practitioner transcends the cycle of birth and death and merges with the divine. The Aghori achieves a state of non-duality, where all dualities are reconciled and the true nature of reality is revealed.

The Role of Darkness in Spiritual Alchemy

In both Luciferianism and Aghora, darkness is not something to be feared or rejected, but an essential part of the alchemical process. Darkness represents the raw, untamed aspects of the self that must be confronted and integrated in order to achieve spiritual transformation. The journey through darkness is often challenging and uncomfortable, but it is necessary for the purification and refinement of the soul.

In Luciferianism, darkness is associated with the shadow—the unconscious, repressed parts of the psyche that must be brought into the light of awareness. The Luciferian path teaches that true enlightenment can only be achieved by confronting and integrating the shadow, embracing the darkness within, and using it as a source of power and wisdom. This process of shadow integration is central to the alchemical transformation of the self, where the practitioner seeks to achieve self-deification and spiritual empowerment.

In Aghora, darkness is embodied in the practices that confront death, impurity, and the profane. The Aghori believes that by engaging with the abject and the terrifying, they can dissolve the ego, transcend duality, and achieve a state of non-duality where all things are seen as expressions of the divine. The journey through darkness in Aghora is marked by intense spiritual practices that challenge societal norms and the limitations of the ego, ultimately leading to spiritual liberation.

The role of darkness in spiritual alchemy is also reflected in the symbolism of the black flame in Luciferianism. The black flame represents the inner divine spark that burns within each individual, a source of power and illumination that emerges from the darkness of the unconscious. By meditating on the black flame and invoking its power, the practitioner seeks to awaken their divine potential and to achieve enlightenment through the integration of both light and dark.

In Aghora, the role of darkness is embodied in the worship of Kali, the dark mother who represents the forces of destruction and creation. Kali's darkness is not a void, but a fertile ground for spiritual growth, where the seed of enlightenment is planted and nurtured. The Aghori seeks to merge with Kali, to become one with her cosmic dance, and to achieve spiritual liberation through the embrace of both creation and destruction.

The Transformation of the Self

The ultimate goal of spiritual alchemy in both Luciferianism and Aghora is the transformation of the self—the process of turning the base elements of the soul into the spiritual gold of enlightenment and self-realization. This transformation involves the purification of the self, the integration of the shadow, and the realization of one's divine potential.

In Luciferianism, the transformation of the self is achieved through the process of self-deification, where the practitioner seeks to become a god unto themselves. This process involves the confrontation and integration of the shadow, the awakening of the black flame, and the realization of the self as a divine being. The Luciferian path teaches that true spiritual empowerment can only be achieved by embracing both light and dark aspects of the self, using the darkness within as a source of power and wisdom.

The transformation of the self in Aghora is achieved through the process of moksha, or spiritual liberation, where the practitioner transcends the cycle of birth and death and merges with the divine. This process involves the dissolution of the ego, the transcendence of duality, and the realization of non-duality, where all things are seen as expressions of the divine. The Aghori path teaches that true spiritual liberation can only be achieved by confronting death, impurity, and the profane, embracing the totality of existence, and surrendering to the divine mother Kali.

Both traditions emphasize the importance of confronting and integrating the shadow as a crucial part of the transformative process. The shadow represents the unconscious, repressed parts of the psyche that must be brought into the light of awareness in order to achieve spiritual enlightenment. The process of shadow integration is not easy; it requires courage, introspection, and a willingness to confront the darkest aspects of the self. But through this process, the practitioner is able to achieve a more complete and powerful state of being, where they are fully aligned with their true will and their divine potential.

The Goal of Spiritual Enlightenment

The ultimate goal of spiritual alchemy in both Luciferianism and Aghora is the attainment of spiritual enlightenment—a state of being where the practitioner realizes their divine nature, transcends duality, and achieves a profound understanding of the mysteries of existence. This goal is achieved through the process of transformation, where the base elements of the self are purified, refined, and elevated to their highest potential.

In Luciferianism, spiritual enlightenment is achieved through the process of self-deification, where the practitioner becomes a god unto themselves, fully in control of their destiny and in possession of profound spiritual insight. This state of enlightenment is marked by a deep sense of inner peace, fulfillment, and empowerment, where the individual is fully aligned with their true will and their divine potential.

In Aghora, spiritual enlightenment is achieved through the attainment of moksha, or spiritual liberation, where the practitioner transcends the cycle of birth and death and merges with the divine. This state of enlightenment is marked by the realization of non-duality, where all distinctions between self and other, life and death, sacred and profane, are reconciled, and the true nature of reality is revealed.

Both traditions emphasize the importance of the journey through darkness as a necessary part of the path to enlightenment. The journey through darkness, whether it involves the confrontation with the shadow in Luciferianism or the embrace of death and impurity in Aghora, is a transformative process that purifies the soul, dissolves the ego, and prepares the practitioner for the final stages of spiritual alchemy.

Conclusion: The Alchemical Path to Enlightenment

The alchemy of the soul is a profound and transformative journey that leads to spiritual enlightenment, self-deification, and liberation. In both Luciferianism and Aghora, this journey involves the purification of the self, the integration of the shadow, and the realization of one's divine potential. The journey through darkness, whether it involves the embrace of the shadow in Luciferianism or the confrontation with death and impurity in Aghora, is a necessary part of the alchemical process, where the base elements of the self are transmuted into the spiritual gold of enlightenment.

As we continue our exploration of the convergence between Aghora and Luciferianism, we will delve into the concept of ego death, examining how both traditions view the dissolution of the ego as a crucial step in the journey towards spiritual enlightenment and self-realization. In the next chapter, we will explore the concept of ego death in both traditions, focusing on the practices and rituals that facilitate this transformative process.

CHAPTER 8: THE DEATH OF THE EGO

The concept of ego death is central to the spiritual paths of both Luciferianism and Aghora. The ego, often seen as the source of attachment, fear, and separation, is perceived as an obstacle to spiritual enlightenment and self-realization. To transcend the limitations imposed by the ego, both traditions emphasize the importance of dissolving the ego, allowing the practitioner to experience a state of non-duality and union with the divine. In this chapter, we will explore the concept of ego death in both traditions, examining the practices and rituals that facilitate this transformative process and the profound implications it has for the spiritual journey.

Understanding the Ego and Its Role in Spiritual Practice

The ego, in psychological and spiritual terms, refers to the sense of self that is defined by individual identity, desires, fears, and attachments. It is the aspect of consciousness that perceives itself as separate from others and from the world, creating a sense of duality that underlies much of human experience. While the ego plays an important role in navigating the material world, it is also seen as a source of suffering, as it perpetuates the illusion of separateness and reinforces attachments to transient, worldly phenomena.

In spiritual practice, the ego is often seen as the primary barrier to enlightenment. The ego clings to identity, status, and material possessions, creating a false sense of self that obscures the true, divine nature of the individual. To achieve spiritual enlightenment, the practitioner must transcend the ego, dissolving the boundaries between self and other, and realizing the underlying unity of all things.

In Luciferianism, the ego is seen as both a tool and an obstacle. On one hand, the ego can be harnessed to achieve self-deification, where the individual asserts their sovereignty and divine potential. On the other hand, the ego's attachments and fears must be confronted and integrated to achieve true spiritual enlightenment. The process of ego death in Luciferianism involves the confrontation with the shadow—the dark, repressed aspects of the self that must be brought into the light of awareness.

In Aghora, the ego is seen as an illusion that must be dissolved to achieve moksha, or spiritual liberation. The Aghori believes that by confronting death, impurity, and the profane, they can dissolve the ego and achieve a state of non-duality where all distinctions between self and other, life and death, are obliterated. The process of ego death in Aghora is marked by intense spiritual practices that challenge the ego's attachments and dissolve the illusion of separateness.

Ego Death in Luciferianism: The Confrontation with the Shadow

In Luciferianism, the process of ego death is closely tied to the concept of shadow integration. The shadow, as described by Carl Jung, represents the unconscious, repressed parts of the psyche—those aspects of the self that are denied, feared, or rejected. The shadow contains both the dark and the potentially positive aspects of the self that have been pushed into the unconscious due to societal or personal conditioning.

The Luciferian path teaches that true spiritual enlightenment can only be achieved by confronting and integrating the shadow. This involves acknowledging the parts of the self that have been repressed, bringing them into the light of awareness, and embracing them as integral aspects of the self. The process of shadow integration is not easy; it requires courage, introspection, and a willingness to confront the darkest aspects of the psyche.

Luciferian rituals that facilitate shadow integration often involve symbolic acts of rebellion, self-empowerment, and the invocation of Lucifer as the light-bringer. These rituals may include meditative practices that focus on the illumination of the shadow, invocations of Lucifer to guide the practitioner through the darkness, and symbolic acts that challenge conventional morality and societal norms. By confronting the shadow and embracing the darkness within, the practitioner seeks to dissolve the ego and achieve a more complete and empowered state of being.

The ego death in Luciferianism is not the annihilation of the self, but rather the transformation of the self. The goal is to achieve self-deification—a state in which the individual becomes a god unto themselves, fully in control of their destiny and in possession of profound spiritual insight. This process of self-deification involves the integration of both light and dark aspects of the self, the dissolution of the ego's attachments and fears, and the realization of the inner divine spark represented by the black flame.

Ego Death in Aghora: The Embrace of Death and Impurity

In Aghora, the process of ego death is facilitated by intense spiritual practices that confront the realities of death, impurity, and the profane. The Aghori believes that by embracing what society deems impure or terrifying, they can dissolve the ego and achieve a state of non-duality where all things are seen as expressions of the divine.

One of the most significant practices in Aghora is meditating in cremation grounds, where the Aghori confronts the impermanence of life and the reality of death. The cremation ground, or *smashan*, is a sacred space where the physical body is reduced to ashes, symbolizing the dissolution of the ego and the return to the formless essence of the divine. By meditating in such a place, surrounded by death and decay, the Aghori seeks to transcend the fear of mortality and dissolve the illusion of separateness.

The use of human remains in rituals, such as smearing the body with ashes or using a skull as a ritual vessel, is another practice that challenges the ego and dissolves the boundaries between self and other, life and death. These acts are not meant to be morbid or grotesque; they are powerful tools for spiritual purification and transformation. By engaging with what is considered impure, the Aghori seeks to dissolve the ego's attachments to identity, status, and the physical body, preparing the soul for the final stages of spiritual liberation.

The worship of Kali, the dark mother who embodies both creation and destruction, is central to the process of ego death in Aghora. Kali's fierce and terrifying aspects represent the forces of destruction that devour the ego and the illusions it creates. The Aghori offers their desires, attachments, and fears to Kali, surrendering completely to her divine power. Through this act of surrender, the Aghori seeks to merge with Kali, to become one with her cosmic dance, and to achieve moksha—a state of spiritual liberation where all dualities are reconciled, and the true nature of reality is revealed.

The Role of Ritual in Facilitating Ego Death

Ritual plays a crucial role in facilitating ego death in both Luciferianism and Aghora. These rituals are not merely symbolic; they are direct, lived experiences that engage the practitioner on multiple levels—physical, emotional, mental, and spiritual. Through ritual, the practitioner is able to access deeper layers of consciousness, confront the shadow aspects of the self, and dissolve the ego's attachments and fears.

In Luciferianism, rituals that facilitate ego death often involve the invocation of Lucifer as the light-bringer and the adversary. These rituals may include acts of rebellion, self-empowerment, and the conscious integration of both light and dark aspects of the self. The goal of these rituals is to dissolve the ego, to awaken the inner divine spark, and to achieve self-deification. By confronting the shadow and embracing the darkness within, the practitioner seeks to dissolve the boundaries of the ego and to achieve a state of spiritual sovereignty where they are fully in control of their destiny.

In Aghora, rituals that facilitate ego death often involve the use of human remains, meditating in cremation grounds, and the worship of Kali. These practices challenge the ego's attachments to identity, status, and the physical body, dissolving the illusion of separateness and preparing the soul for spiritual liberation. The Aghori seeks to dissolve the ego by embracing what society deems impure or terrifying, merging with the divine through acts of surrender, devotion, and transgression.

Both traditions emphasize the importance of confronting and integrating the shadow as a crucial part of the process of ego death. The shadow represents the unconscious, repressed parts of the psyche that must be brought into the light of awareness in order to achieve spiritual enlightenment. The process of shadow integration is not easy; it requires courage, introspection, and a willingness to confront the darkest aspects of the self. But through this process, the practitioner is able to achieve a more complete and powerful state of being, where they are fully aligned with their true will and their divine potential.

The Experience of Ego Death and Its Implications for Spiritual Enlightenment

The experience of ego death is often described as a profound and transformative moment on the spiritual journey. It is a moment of surrender, where the boundaries of the self dissolve, and the practitioner experiences a state of oneness with the divine. This experience is often accompanied by a sense of inner peace, fulfillment, and a deep understanding of the mysteries of existence.

In Luciferianism, the experience of ego death is often accompanied by the realization of the self as a divine being. The practitioner achieves self-deification, where they are fully in control of their destiny and in possession of profound spiritual insight. This state of enlightenment is marked by a deep sense of inner peace, fulfillment, and empowerment, where the individual is fully aligned with their true will and their divine potential.

In Aghora, the experience of ego death is often accompanied by the attainment of moksha, or spiritual liberation. The Aghori transcends the cycle of birth and death, merging with the divine and achieving a state of non-duality where all distinctions between self and other, life and death, sacred and profane are reconciled. This state of enlightenment is marked by the realization of the true nature of reality, where all things are seen as expressions of the divine mother Kali.

The experience of ego death has profound implications for spiritual enlightenment. By dissolving the ego, the practitioner is able to transcend the limitations of individual identity, fears, and attachments, and to achieve a state of spiritual sovereignty where they are fully in control of their destiny. This state of enlightenment is not the annihilation of the self, but the realization of the self as a divine being, fully aligned with the true will and the divine potential.

Conclusion: The Death of the Ego as a Gateway to Enlightenment

The death of the ego is a crucial step in the journey towards spiritual enlightenment and self-realization in both Luciferianism and Aghora. Through the process of ego death, the practitioner confronts and integrates the shadow, dissolves the boundaries of the self, and experiences a state of oneness with the divine. This transformative process is facilitated by rituals that challenge the ego's attachments and fears, preparing the soul for the final stages of spiritual alchemy and the attainment of enlightenment.

As we continue our exploration of the convergence between Aghora and Luciferianism, we will delve into the concept of rebirth, examining how both traditions view the process of spiritual renewal and the emergence of the enlightened self. In the next chapter, we will explore the concept of spiritual rebirth in both traditions, focusing on the practices and rituals that facilitate this process and the profound implications it has for the spiritual journey.

CHAPTER 9: THE REBIRTH OF THE SELF

The concept of spiritual rebirth is a central theme in many mystical and esoteric traditions, symbolizing the renewal and transformation of the self after the death of the ego. In both Luciferianism and Aghora, the process of rebirth represents the emergence of the enlightened self, a state in which the individual has transcended the limitations of the ego and achieved a deeper understanding of their divine nature. This chapter will explore the concept of spiritual rebirth in both traditions, focusing on the practices and rituals that facilitate this process and the profound implications it has for the spiritual journey.

The Symbolism of Rebirth in Spiritual Traditions

Rebirth, or the renewal of the self, is a powerful symbol in spiritual traditions across the world.

It represents the idea that after a period of transformation—often involving the metaphorical or literal death of the old self—a new, enlightened self emerges, purified and empowered. This concept is often linked to the cycles of nature, such as the changing of the seasons, where death and decay in autumn and winter give way to new growth and life in spring.

In spiritual traditions, rebirth is often associated with the idea of a second birth, a transformation that takes place on a deeper, more spiritual level than the physical birth. This second birth is marked by a profound shift in consciousness, where the individual transcends the limitations of the ego and awakens to a higher understanding of their true nature.

In Luciferianism, rebirth is symbolized by the awakening of the inner divine spark, the black flame that represents the individual's potential for self-deification and spiritual sovereignty. The process of rebirth in Luciferianism involves the dissolution of the ego, the integration of the shadow, and the realization of the self as a divine being. This transformation is not merely symbolic; it is a lived experience that fundamentally changes the practitioner's perception of themselves and the world.

In Aghora, rebirth is symbolized by the attainment

of moksha, or spiritual liberation, where the individual transcends the cycle of birth and death and merges with the divine. The process of rebirth in Aghora involves the dissolution of the ego, the confrontation with death and impurity, and the realization of non-duality, where all distinctions between self and other, life and death, are reconciled.

The Process of Rebirth in Luciferianism

In Luciferianism, the process of rebirth is closely tied to the concept of self-deification, where the practitioner seeks to become a god unto themselves, fully in control of their destiny and in possession of profound spiritual insight. This process involves several key stages, each of which represents a deeper level of transformation and spiritual awakening.

The first stage of rebirth in Luciferianism involves the dissolution of the ego, the aspect of the self that clings to identity, status, and material attachments. This stage is marked by the confrontation with the shadow, where the practitioner must acknowledge and integrate the repressed, denied, or feared aspects of the psyche. Through this process of shadow integration, the practitioner dissolves the boundaries of the ego and prepares for the next stage of spiritual transformation.

The second stage of rebirth involves the awakening of the black flame, the inner divine spark that represents the individual's potential for self-deification. This stage is often marked by a profound shift in consciousness, where the practitioner begins to realize their divine nature and to see themselves as a manifestation of the divine. The black flame symbolizes the light of Lucifer, the morning star, who guides the seeker through the darkness of ignorance and fear and into the light of knowledge and wisdom.

The third stage of rebirth involves the realization of the self as a divine being, fully in control of their destiny and in possession of profound spiritual insight. This stage is marked by the achievement of self-deification, where the practitioner becomes a god unto themselves, fully aligned with their true will and their divine potential. This state of enlightenment is not the end of the spiritual journey but the beginning of a new chapter, where the practitioner uses their divine power to shape their reality and to pursue their highest goals.

Luciferian rituals that facilitate the process of rebirth often involve the invocation of Lucifer as the light-bringer and the adversary. These rituals may include meditative practices that focus on the illumination of the path, symbolic acts that represent the death of the old self, and the awakening of the new, divine self. The practitioner may also engage in rituals that challenge conventional morality and societal norms, using these acts of rebellion as a means of asserting their spiritual sovereignty and their divine nature.

The Process of Rebirth in Aghora

In Aghora, the process of rebirth is closely tied to the attainment of moksha, or spiritual liberation, where the individual transcends the cycle of birth and death and merges with the divine. This process involves several key stages, each of which represents a deeper level of spiritual purification and transformation.

The first stage of rebirth in Aghora involves the dissolution of the ego, the aspect of the self that clings to identity, status, and material attachments. This stage is marked by intense spiritual practices that confront the realities of death, impurity, and the profane. By meditating in cremation grounds, using human remains in rituals, and worshiping Kali, the Aghori seeks to dissolve the ego and prepare the soul for the next stage of spiritual transformation.

The second stage of rebirth involves the realization of non-duality, where the practitioner transcends the distinctions between self and other, life and death, sacred and profane. This stage is often marked by a profound shift in consciousness, where the Aghori begins to see all things as expressions of the divine, and the illusion of separateness is dissolved. The practitioner experiences a state of oneness with the divine, where all dualities are reconciled, and the true nature of reality is revealed.

The third stage of rebirth involves the attainment of moksha, where the practitioner achieves spiritual liberation and merges with the divine. This stage is marked by the complete dissolution of the ego, the transcendence of the cycle of birth and death, and the realization of the self as an expression of the divine mother Kali. The Aghori experiences a state of inner peace, fulfillment, and spiritual sovereignty, where they are fully aligned with the divine will and the cosmic order.

Aghori rituals that facilitate the process of rebirth often involve acts of surrender, devotion, and transgression. These rituals may include offerings to Kali, meditations on death and impurity, and symbolic acts that represent the dissolution of the old self and the emergence of the new, enlightened self. The Aghori uses these rituals to dissolve the ego, to transcend duality, and to achieve a state of spiritual liberation where they are fully merged with the divine.

The Role of Ritual in Facilitating Rebirth

Ritual plays a crucial role in facilitating the process

of rebirth in both Luciferianism and Aghora. These rituals are not merely symbolic; they are direct, lived experiences that engage the practitioner on multiple levels—physical, emotional, mental, and spiritual. Through ritual, the practitioner is able to access deeper layers of consciousness, to dissolve the old self, and to awaken to a new, enlightened state of being.

In Luciferianism, rituals that facilitate rebirth often involve the invocation of Lucifer as the light-bringer, the integration of the shadow, and the awakening of the black flame. These rituals may include meditative practices that focus on the illumination of the path, symbolic acts that represent the death of the old self, and the realization of the new, divine self. The practitioner uses these rituals to dissolve the ego, to awaken their divine potential, and to achieve self-deification.

In Aghora, rituals that facilitate rebirth often involve the worship of Kali, the confrontation with death and impurity, and the realization of non-duality. These rituals may include offerings to Kali, meditations in cremation grounds, and symbolic acts that represent the dissolution of the old self and the emergence of the new, enlightened self. The Aghori uses these rituals to dissolve the ego, to transcend duality, and to achieve moksha, where they are fully merged with the divine.

Both traditions emphasize the importance of the death of the old self as a necessary step in the process of rebirth. The old self, with its attachments, fears, and limitations, must be dissolved to make way for the new, enlightened self. This process of dissolution and renewal is facilitated by ritual, where the practitioner engages in symbolic acts that represent the death of the ego and the awakening of the divine self.

The Experience of Rebirth and Its Implications for the Spiritual Journey

The experience of rebirth is often described as a profound and transformative moment on the spiritual journey. It is a moment of awakening, where the boundaries of the old self dissolve, and the practitioner experiences a state of oneness with the divine. This experience is often accompanied by a sense of inner peace, fulfillment, and a deep understanding of the mysteries of existence.

In Luciferianism, the experience of rebirth is often accompanied by the realization of the self as a divine being. The practitioner achieves self-deification, where they are fully in control of their destiny and in possession of profound spiritual insight. This state of enlightenment is marked by a deep sense of inner peace, fulfillment, and empowerment, where the individual is fully aligned with their true will and their divine potential.

In Aghora, the experience of rebirth is often accompanied by the attainment of moksha, where the practitioner transcends the cycle of birth and death and merges with the divine. The Aghori experiences a state of inner peace, fulfillment, and spiritual sovereignty, where they are fully aligned with the divine will and the cosmic order. This state of enlightenment is marked by the realization of the true nature of reality, where all things are seen as expressions of the divine mother Kali.

The experience of rebirth has profound implications for the spiritual journey. By dissolving the old self and awakening to a new, enlightened state of being, the practitioner is able to transcend the limitations of individual identity, fears, and attachments, and to achieve a state of spiritual sovereignty where they are fully in control of their destiny. This state of enlightenment is not the end of the spiritual journey but the beginning of a new chapter, where the practitioner uses their divine power to shape their reality and to pursue their highest goals.

Conclusion: The Rebirth of the Self as a Gateway to Enlightenment

The rebirth of the self is a crucial step in the journey towards spiritual enlightenment and self-realization in both Luciferianism and Aghora.

Through the process of rebirth, the practitioner dissolves the old self, awakens to a new, enlightened state of being, and achieves a profound understanding of their divine nature. This transformative process is facilitated by rituals that challenge the ego, dissolve attachments and fears, and prepare the soul for the final stages of spiritual alchemy and the attainment of enlightenment.

As we continue our exploration of the convergence between Aghora and Luciferianism, we will delve into the concept of spiritual sovereignty, examining how both traditions view the attainment of spiritual power and the realization of the divine self. In the next chapter, we will explore the concept of spiritual sovereignty in both traditions, focusing on the practices and rituals that facilitate this process and the profound implications it has for the spiritual journey.

CHAPTER 10: SPIRITUAL SOVEREIGNTY

Spiritual sovereignty is the ultimate realization of the divine self, where the practitioner becomes fully autonomous, self-empowered, and aligned with their true will. In both Luciferianism and Aghora, spiritual sovereignty is the culmination of the transformative processes of ego death and rebirth. It represents the state in which the practitioner has transcended the limitations of the ego, integrated both light and dark aspects of the self, and attained a profound understanding of their divine nature. This chapter will explore the concept of spiritual sovereignty in both traditions, examining the practices and rituals that facilitate this process and the profound implications it has for the spiritual journey.

The Concept of Spiritual Sovereignty

Spiritual sovereignty is the state of being in which the individual is fully in control of their destiny, free from external influences, and aligned with their highest spiritual purpose. It is a state of self-mastery, where the practitioner has transcended the dualities of light and dark, good and evil, sacred and profane, and recognizes themselves as a manifestation of the divine. In this state, the practitioner is no longer bound by the limitations of the ego, but operates from a place of spiritual authority, wisdom, and power.

In Luciferianism, spiritual sovereignty is closely tied to the concept of self-deification, where the practitioner seeks to become a god unto themselves. This involves the full realization of the black flame—the inner divine spark that represents the individual's potential for spiritual empowerment and enlightenment. Spiritual sovereignty in Luciferianism is not about worshipping an external deity, but about recognizing and actualizing the divine potential within oneself.

In Aghora, spiritual sovereignty is achieved through the attainment of moksha, where the practitioner transcends the cycle of birth and death and merges with the divine. This state is marked by the complete dissolution of the ego and the realization of non-duality, where all distinctions between self and other, life and death, are obliterated. The Aghori operates from a place of spiritual sovereignty, fully aligned with the cosmic order and the divine will, recognizing themselves as an expression of the goddess Kali.

Spiritual sovereignty is not just a philosophical concept; it is a lived experience that profoundly changes the practitioner's perception of themselves and the world. It involves a deep understanding of the nature of reality, the recognition of one's divine potential, and the ability to manifest one's will in alignment with the highest spiritual truths.

The Path to Spiritual Sovereignty in Luciferianism

In Luciferianism, the path to spiritual sovereignty involves several key stages, each of which represents a deeper level of transformation and self-realization. These stages are facilitated by practices and rituals that challenge the ego, integrate the shadow, and awaken the black flame.

The first stage involves the confrontation and integration of the shadow, where the practitioner must acknowledge and embrace the repressed, denied, or feared aspects of the psyche. This process dissolves the boundaries of the ego and prepares the individual for the next stage of spiritual empowerment.

The second stage involves the awakening of the black flame, the inner divine spark that represents the practitioner's potential for self-deification. This stage is marked by a profound shift in consciousness, where the individual begins to see themselves as a manifestation of the divine, fully in control of their destiny. The black flame symbolizes the light of Lucifer, the morning star, who guides the seeker through the darkness and into the light of knowledge and wisdom.

The third stage involves the full realization of spiritual sovereignty, where the practitioner becomes a god unto themselves. This state is marked by a deep sense of inner peace, fulfillment, and empowerment, where the individual is fully aligned with their true will and their divine potential. The practitioner uses their spiritual power to shape their reality, manifest their highest goals, and operate from a place of spiritual authority.

Luciferian rituals that facilitate the attainment of spiritual sovereignty often involve the invocation of Lucifer as the light-bringer and the adversary. These rituals may include meditative practices that focus on the illumination of the path, symbolic acts of rebellion and self-empowerment, and the conscious integration of both light and dark aspects of the self. The practitioner may also engage in rituals that challenge conventional morality and societal norms, using these acts of transgression as a means of asserting their spiritual sovereignty and divine nature.

The attainment of spiritual sovereignty in Luciferianism is not about dominating others or exerting external power, but about mastering oneself, aligning with the true will, and recognizing the divine potential within. It is a state of inner authority, where the practitioner operates from a place of spiritual wisdom and power, fully in control of their destiny and fully aligned with the highest spiritual truths.

The Path to Spiritual Sovereignty in Aghora

In Aghora, the path to spiritual sovereignty is achieved through the attainment of moksha, where the practitioner transcends the cycle of birth and death and merges with the divine. This path involves several key stages, each of which represents a deeper level of spiritual purification, transformation, and self-realization.

The first stage involves the dissolution of the ego, the aspect of the self that clings to identity, status, and material attachments. This stage is marked by intense spiritual practices that confront the realities of death, impurity, and the profane. By meditating in cremation grounds, using human remains in rituals, and worshipping Kali, the

Aghori seeks to dissolve the ego and prepare the soul for the next stage of spiritual sovereignty.

The second stage involves the realization of non-duality, where the practitioner transcends the distinctions between self and other, life and death, sacred and profane. This stage is marked by a profound shift in consciousness, where the Aghori begins to see all things as expressions of the divine, and the illusion of separateness is dissolved. The practitioner operates from a place of spiritual sovereignty, fully aligned with the cosmic order and the divine will.

The third stage involves the attainment of moksha, where the practitioner achieves spiritual liberation and merges with the divine. This state is marked by the complete dissolution of the ego, the transcendence of the cycle of birth and death, and the realization of the self as an expression of the goddess Kali. The Aghori operates from a place of spiritual sovereignty, fully aligned with the divine will and the cosmic order, recognizing themselves as an embodiment of the divine mother.

Aghori rituals that facilitate the attainment of spiritual sovereignty often involve acts of surrender, devotion, and transgression. These rituals may include offerings to Kali, meditations on death and impurity, and symbolic acts that represent the dissolution of the ego and the realization of the divine self. The Aghori uses these rituals to dissolve the ego, to transcend duality, and to achieve a state of spiritual sovereignty where they are fully merged with the divine.

The attainment of spiritual sovereignty in Aghora is not about asserting external power, but about recognizing and embodying the divine within. It is a state of inner authority, where the practitioner operates from a place of spiritual wisdom and alignment with the cosmic order. The Aghori recognizes that they are not separate from the divine, but are an expression of the divine mother Kali, fully aligned with her will and fully merged with her cosmic dance.

The Role of Ritual in Attaining Spiritual Sovereignty

Ritual plays a crucial role in attaining spiritual sovereignty in both Luciferianism and Aghora. These rituals are not merely symbolic; they are direct, lived experiences that engage the practitioner on multiple levels—physical, emotional, mental, and spiritual. Through ritual, the practitioner is able to access deeper layers of consciousness, to dissolve the ego, and to awaken to a state of spiritual sovereignty.

In Luciferianism, rituals that facilitate spiritual sovereignty often involve the invocation of Lucifer as the light-bringer, the integration of the shadow, and the awakening of the black flame. These rituals may include meditative practices that focus on the illumination of the path, symbolic acts of rebellion and self-empowerment, and the conscious integration of both light and dark aspects of the self. The practitioner uses these rituals to dissolve the ego, to awaken their divine potential, and to achieve self-deification.

In Aghora, rituals that facilitate spiritual sovereignty often involve the worship of Kali, the confrontation with death and impurity, and the realization of non-duality. These rituals may include offerings to Kali, meditations in cremation grounds, and symbolic acts that represent the dissolution of the ego and the emergence of the divine self. The Aghori uses these rituals to dissolve the ego, to transcend duality, and to achieve moksha, where they are fully merged with the divine.

Both traditions emphasize the importance of the death of the ego and the realization of the divine self as necessary steps in attaining spiritual sovereignty. The ego, with its attachments, fears, and limitations, must be dissolved to make way for the divine self, fully aligned with the true will and the highest spiritual truths. This process of dissolution and renewal is facilitated by ritual, where the practitioner engages in symbolic acts that represent the death of the old self and the awakening of the new, enlightened self.

The Experience of Spiritual Sovereignty and Its Implications for the Spiritual Journey

The experience of spiritual sovereignty is often described as a profound and transformative moment on the spiritual journey. It is a moment of awakening, where the boundaries of the old self dissolve, and the practitioner experiences a state of oneness with the divine. This experience is often accompanied by a sense of inner peace, fulfillment, and a deep understanding of the mysteries of existence.

In Luciferianism, the experience of spiritual sovereignty is often accompanied by the realization of the self as a divine being. The practitioner achieves self-deification, where they are fully in control of their destiny and in possession of profound spiritual insight. This state of enlightenment is marked by a deep sense of inner peace, fulfillment, and empowerment, where the individual is fully aligned with their true will and their divine potential.

In Aghora, the experience of spiritual sovereignty is often accompanied by the attainment of moksha, where the practitioner transcends the cycle of birth and death and merges with the divine. The Aghori experiences a state of inner peace, fulfillment, and spiritual sovereignty, where they are fully aligned with the divine will and the cosmic order. This state of enlightenment is marked by the realization of the true nature of reality, where all things are seen as expressions of the divine mother Kali.

The experience of spiritual sovereignty has profound implications for the spiritual journey. By dissolving the old self and awakening to a new, enlightened state of being, the practitioner is able to transcend the limitations of individual identity, fears, and attachments, and to achieve a state of spiritual sovereignty where they are fully in control of their destiny. This state of enlightenment is not the end of the spiritual journey but the beginning of a new chapter, where the practitioner uses their divine power to shape their reality and to pursue their highest goals.

Conclusion: Spiritual Sovereignty as the Culmination of the Spiritual Journey

Spiritual sovereignty is the culmination of the spiritual journey in both Luciferianism and Aghora. Through the processes of ego death, rebirth, and the realization of the divine self, the practitioner achieves a state of self-mastery, spiritual empowerment, and alignment with the highest spiritual truths. This state of spiritual sovereignty is not about external power or domination, but about mastering oneself, recognizing the divine within, and operating from a place of spiritual authority, wisdom, and power.

As we continue our exploration of the convergence between Aghora and Luciferianism, we will delve into the final chapter, where we will explore the integration of these teachings into everyday life, examining how the principles of spiritual sovereignty, non-duality, and the divine self can be applied to the challenges and opportunities of the modern world. In the next chapter, we will explore how to live as a spiritually sovereign being, fully aligned with the highest spiritual truths and fully empowered to manifest one's true will in the world.

CHAPTER 11: LIVING AS A SPIRITUALLY SOVEREIGN BEING

With the attainment of spiritual sovereignty comes the challenge of integrating these profound insights and powers into everyday life. The journey of transformation, from the dissolution of the ego to the realization of the divine self, is not complete until these principles are embodied in daily actions, decisions, and interactions with the world. This final chapter explores how the teachings of Luciferianism and Aghora can be applied to the practical aspects of life, guiding the practitioner to live as a spiritually sovereign being fully aligned with their true will and the highest spiritual truths.

The Principles of Spiritual Sovereignty in Everyday Life

Living as a spiritually sovereign being involves more than just understanding or intellectualizing spiritual principles; it requires the embodiment of those principles in every aspect of life. This embodiment means that the insights gained through the journey of ego death, rebirth, and the realization of the divine self must influence how one thinks, feels, and acts in the world.

1. **Alignment with True Will:**
   One of the core principles of spiritual sovereignty is alignment with true will—the deep, inner sense of purpose that arises from the realization of one's divine nature. True will is not driven by egoic desires or societal expectations but is rooted in the highest spiritual truths. Living in alignment with true will means making decisions that reflect this deeper purpose, pursuing goals that are in harmony with one's spiritual path, and resisting the temptations of distractions or diversions that lead away from spiritual growth.

   In practical terms, this might involve setting clear intentions for one's life, career, and relationships that are aligned with one's spiritual goals. It might also involve making difficult choices that require letting go of attachments, fears, or societal pressures in order to stay true to one's path.

2. **Integration of Light and Dark:**
A spiritually sovereign being recognizes that both light and dark are essential aspects of the self and the cosmos. This integration involves accepting and embracing all parts of oneself, including the shadow, and using the insights gained from this integration to navigate the challenges of life. It means acknowledging the complexities of human experience, without falling into dualistic thinking that separates good from bad, right from wrong, or sacred from profane.

Practically, this might involve approaching conflicts or challenges with a balanced perspective, understanding that difficulties often contain valuable lessons, and that embracing both success and failure can lead to greater wisdom. It also means maintaining compassion for oneself and others, recognizing that all beings are on their own unique spiritual journeys.

3. **Self-Mastery and Discipline:**
Spiritual sovereignty requires a high degree of self-mastery and discipline. This

means cultivating the inner strength to control one's thoughts, emotions, and actions, rather than being controlled by them. It involves developing the ability to respond to situations with wisdom and discernment, rather than reacting out of habit or impulse. Self-mastery also includes the discipline to maintain spiritual practices that support ongoing growth and alignment with true will.

In daily life, this could manifest as a commitment to regular meditation, mindfulness practices, or rituals that keep the mind and spirit attuned to the divine. It might also involve setting boundaries, making conscious choices about how to spend time and energy, and staying focused on long-term spiritual goals rather than short-term gratification.

4. **Manifestation of Divine Power:**

A spiritually sovereign being recognizes their ability to manifest their will in the world, drawing upon the divine power within. This manifestation is not about controlling or dominating others but about bringing one's highest visions and intentions into reality in a way that benefits oneself and others. It involves using one's spiritual insights and powers to create positive change, to uplift others, and to contribute to the greater good.

Practically, this could involve setting goals that reflect one's highest spiritual aspirations, using visualization, affirmations, or other manifestation techniques to bring these goals into reality, and taking inspired action to make them happen. It might also involve using one's influence, talents, or resources to support causes or projects that align with one's spiritual values.

5. **Service to the Divine:**

Spiritual sovereignty is not just about personal empowerment; it is also about service to the divine. This service involves recognizing that one's life is part of a larger cosmic order, and that true fulfillment comes from aligning one's will with the will of the divine. Service to the divine might involve acts of compassion, generosity, or selflessness, as well as a commitment to living in harmony with the natural world and all beings.

In daily life, this could manifest as a commitment to ethical living, making choices that reflect respect for the earth and all its inhabitants, and engaging in acts of kindness, charity, or service that contribute to the well-being of others. It might also involve cultivating a deep sense of gratitude for the gift of life and the opportunity to grow spiritually.

Practical Applications of Spiritual Sovereignty

The principles of spiritual sovereignty can be applied to all areas of life, from personal relationships to career, health, and community involvement. Here are some examples of how these principles might be practically applied:

- **Relationships:**
  In relationships, spiritual sovereignty involves recognizing the divine in oneself and in others, and relating to others from a place of respect, compassion, and integrity. It means setting healthy boundaries, communicating clearly and honestly, and choosing relationships that support mutual growth and alignment with true will. It also involves letting go of relationships that no longer serve one's highest good, with love and gratitude for the lessons they have provided.

- **Career:**
  In one's career, spiritual sovereignty involves pursuing work that aligns with one's true will and spiritual values. This might mean choosing a profession that allows for creative expression, service to others, or personal growth. It also means bringing integrity, discipline, and a commitment to excellence to one's work,

recognizing that all work can be a form of spiritual practice if approached with the right mindset.
- **Health and Well-being:**
Spiritual sovereignty includes taking responsibility for one's physical, mental, and emotional well-being. This involves making choices that support a healthy, balanced lifestyle, such as eating nourishing foods, engaging in regular physical activity, and practicing mindfulness or stress-reduction techniques. It also means recognizing the importance of self-care and rest, and not allowing external pressures to compromise one's health or well-being.
- **Community and Social Involvement:**
As a spiritually sovereign being, one recognizes the importance of contributing to the greater good and being of service to others. This might involve participating in community activities, supporting causes that align with one's values, or using one's influence or resources to create positive change. It also means acting with integrity and compassion in all interactions, recognizing that each action has an impact on the collective whole.
- **Spiritual Practice:**
Finally, spiritual sovereignty involves maintaining a regular spiritual practice that supports ongoing growth and alignment with

true will. This might include meditation, ritual, prayer, or other forms of spiritual discipline that keep the mind and spirit attuned to the divine. It also means staying open to new insights, teachings, and experiences that support continued spiritual evolution.

Challenges and Opportunities of Living as a Spiritually Sovereign Being

Living as a spiritually sovereign being is not without its challenges. It requires a high degree of self-awareness, discipline, and commitment to one's spiritual path. It also requires the courage to make difficult choices, to let go of attachments, and to navigate the complexities of life with wisdom and discernment.

One of the challenges of spiritual sovereignty is maintaining alignment with true will in the face of external pressures, distractions, or temptations. This might involve making choices that are unpopular or misunderstood by others, or staying true to one's path even when it is difficult or uncomfortable. It also involves navigating the balance between personal empowerment and humility, recognizing that spiritual sovereignty is not about egoic pride but about service to the divine.

Another challenge is integrating the light and dark aspects of the self in a way that is balanced and harmonious. This involves acknowledging and embracing all parts of oneself, without falling into extremes of self-criticism or self-indulgence. It also means recognizing the potential for both light and dark within others, and relating to them from a place of compassion and understanding.

However, the opportunities of living as a spiritually sovereign being are immense. It allows for a life of deep fulfillment, inner peace, and alignment with the highest spiritual truths. It provides the foundation for manifesting one's true will in the world, for creating positive change, and for experiencing the profound joy of being fully aligned with one's divine nature.

Conclusion: The Journey Continues

The attainment of spiritual sovereignty is not the end of the spiritual journey but the beginning of a new chapter. It represents the culmination of the transformative processes of ego death, rebirth, and the realization of the divine self, but it also opens the door to new challenges, opportunities, and experiences. As a spiritually sovereign being, one is called to live in alignment with true will, to manifest divine power in the world, and to serve the greater good with wisdom, compassion, and integrity.

The teachings of Luciferianism and Aghora provide powerful tools for navigating this journey, offering insights and practices that support the realization of spiritual sovereignty and the integration of these principles into everyday life. By embracing the full spectrum of human experience—light and dark, sacred and profane, life and death—one can achieve a state of inner peace, fulfillment, and spiritual empowerment that transcends the limitations of the ego and aligns with the highest spiritual truths.

As we conclude this exploration of the convergence between Aghora and Luciferianism, it is clear that both traditions offer profound insights into the nature of the self, the divine, and the path to enlightenment. By integrating these teachings into everyday life, one can live as a spiritually sovereign being, fully aligned with the true will and fully empowered to create a life of meaning, purpose, and spiritual fulfillment.

CHAPTER 12: SUGGESTED RITUALS, MEDITATIONS, AND EXERCISES

This expanded appendix offers a more detailed exploration of rituals, meditations, and exercises for readers who wish to deepen their practice of Luciferianism and Aghora. Each practice is designed to support the transformative processes of ego death, shadow integration, spiritual rebirth, and the attainment of spiritual sovereignty.

1. The Shadow Integration Ritual

Purpose:
To confront and integrate the shadow aspects of the self, bringing unconscious fears, desires, and repressed traits into conscious awareness. This

ritual helps the practitioner embrace the full spectrum of their being, leading to greater self-understanding and empowerment.

Materials:

- A black candle
- A mirror
- A journal and pen
- A quiet space where you won't be disturbed
- Incense (optional)
- A small bowl of water (symbolizing purification)

Instructions:

1. **Preparation:**
   Find a quiet space where you can perform this ritual without interruption. Light the black candle and place it in front of the mirror. Light the incense if you are using it, and place the bowl of water nearby. The water represents the potential for purification and healing during this process.

2. **Meditation:**
   Sit comfortably and take a few deep breaths. Focus on the flame of the candle, allowing its light to relax your mind and body. As you gaze into the flame, begin to visualize the aspects of yourself that you consider to be part of your shadow—fears,

repressed desires, or traits you've denied. Allow these aspects to come into your awareness without judgment.

3. **Reflection:**
Look into the mirror and gaze into your own eyes. As you do, speak aloud or silently the aspects of your shadow that you wish to confront. For example: "I acknowledge my fear of failure," "I recognize my repressed anger," or "I accept my desire for power." As you name each aspect, see it reflected back to you in the mirror, acknowledging it as a part of yourself.

4. **Integration:**
As you continue to gaze into the mirror, affirm that these aspects are part of you and that you accept them without judgment. Say, "I embrace my shadow as a part of my whole self." Visualize the light of the candle illuminating these shadow aspects, bringing them into your conscious awareness. Imagine the light filling your entire being, integrating these aspects into a harmonious whole.

5. **Purification:**
Dip your fingers into the bowl of water and touch your forehead, heart, and abdomen, symbolizing the purification of your thoughts, emotions, and instincts. As you

do, say, "I purify my shadow with the light of awareness. I accept and integrate all parts of myself." Feel the water cleansing any residual negativity or resistance.

6. **Journaling:**
After the ritual, take time to journal about your experience. Write down the aspects of your shadow that you confronted, how you felt during the ritual, and any insights you gained. Reflect on how you can integrate these aspects into your daily life in a healthy and balanced way. Consider setting intentions for how you will work with these aspects moving forward.

7. **Closing:**
Extinguish the candle and incense (if used) and close the ritual with a moment of gratitude for the insights gained. Commit to revisiting this practice regularly to deepen your understanding of the shadow and continue the process of integration.

8. **Optional Extension:**
If you feel called to deepen this practice, consider creating a piece of art, writing a poem, or engaging in another form of creative expression that represents your shadow. Use this creative process as a way to further explore and integrate the shadow aspects you have identified.

2. The Black Flame Meditation

Purpose:

To awaken and nurture the black flame within—the inner divine spark that represents your potential for self-deification and spiritual sovereignty. This meditation helps the practitioner connect with their inner power and divine essence.

Materials:

- A dark, quiet room
- A black or dark-colored candle
- A comfortable seat or cushion
- A small crystal or gemstone (optional, to amplify focus)

Instructions:

1. **Preparation:**
   Find a dark, quiet room where you can meditate without disturbance. Light the black candle and place it in front of you at eye level. If you are using a crystal or gemstone, hold it in your hand or place it in front of the candle. Sit comfortably and close your eyes for a few moments, focusing on your breath.

2. **Grounding:**
   Begin by grounding yourself. Visualize roots extending from your feet into the earth, anchoring you firmly in place. Feel

the energy of the earth rising up through these roots, filling you with stability and strength.

3. **Visualization:**
Open your eyes and gaze at the flame. As you do, visualize a black flame burning within your heart or solar plexus. See this flame as a source of inner power, wisdom, and divine potential. Imagine it flickering and growing stronger with each breath, filling you with warmth and light.

4. **Mantra:**
As you continue to meditate on the black flame, silently repeat the mantra: "I am the light in the darkness. I awaken the divine spark within me." With each repetition, feel the flame within you growing brighter and more powerful, illuminating every part of your being.

5. **Deepening the Connection:**
As you deepen your connection with the black flame, imagine it expanding beyond your body, enveloping you in a protective and empowering aura. Feel this aura as a shield that reflects your inner strength and sovereignty. If you are holding a crystal or gemstone, imagine it absorbing and amplifying the energy of the black flame.

6. **Exploring the Flame's Power:**
Take a moment to explore the qualities of

the black flame. What does it represent for you? How does it feel to be connected to this inner source of power? Reflect on how you can use this power in your life to overcome challenges, manifest your true will, and navigate the path of spiritual sovereignty.

7. **Affirmation:**
Continue to meditate on the black flame for 10-15 minutes, repeating your mantra and allowing the energy of the flame to fill you with a sense of empowerment and spiritual sovereignty. Affirm your connection to this divine spark by saying, "I am a sovereign being, guided by the light within."

8. **Integration:**
After the meditation, sit quietly for a few moments and reflect on the experience. Consider how you can carry this sense of empowerment and divine potential into your daily life. How can you embody the qualities of the black flame in your interactions, decisions, and spiritual practices?

9. **Closing:**
Extinguish the candle and carry the sense of the black flame with you as you go about your day, using it as a reminder of your inner strength and spiritual sovereignty. If

you used a crystal or gemstone, you may choose to carry it with you or place it on your altar as a symbol of your connection to the black flame.

10. **Optional Extension:**
    To deepen this practice, consider incorporating the black flame meditation into your daily routine. You can also explore variations of this meditation by focusing on different aspects of the black flame, such as its connection to wisdom, protection, or creative power.

3. The Smashan Meditation

Purpose:

To confront the impermanence of life and the reality of death, dissolving the ego and preparing for spiritual liberation. This meditation helps the practitioner embrace the natural cycles of life and death and develop a deeper understanding of the transient nature of existence.

Materials:

- A quiet outdoor space (a forest, park, or backyard) or a space where you feel connected to nature
- A blanket or cushion to sit on
- A small offering (such as flowers, fruit, or incense) for the earth (optional)
- A mala or prayer beads (optional)

Instructions:

1. **Preparation:**
   Find a quiet outdoor space where you can meditate without interruption. Sit comfortably on your blanket or cushion and close your eyes. If you have a small offering, place it on the ground in front of you as a gesture of gratitude to the earth.

2. **Connection to Nature:**
   Take a few deep breaths, feeling the ground beneath you and the air around you. Imagine yourself surrounded by the natural cycles of life and death—the growth and decay of plants, the changing of the seasons, and the endless renewal of nature. Acknowledge the earth as both the giver and receiver of life.

3. **Grounding and Centering:**
   Begin by grounding yourself in the present moment. Imagine roots extending from your body into the earth, anchoring you to the soil beneath you. Feel the earth's energy rising up through these roots, filling you with stability and calm. If you are using a mala or prayer beads, you may choose to hold them in your hand as you meditate.

4. **Visualization:**
   As you meditate, visualize yourself sitting

in a cremation ground, surrounded by the ashes of the dead. Imagine the smoke rising from the cremation pyres, carrying the souls of the departed to the next realm. Reflect on the impermanence of life and the inevitability of death. Allow these reflections to deepen your awareness of the transient nature of all things.

5. **Ego Dissolution:**
As you continue to meditate, imagine your own body dissolving into the earth, your ego fading away like the smoke from the pyres. Repeat silently or aloud: "I dissolve the ego. I return to the earth. I am one with the divine." Feel yourself merging with the earth, becoming one with the cycles of life and death.

6. **Mantra Recitation (Optional):**
If you are using a mala or prayer beads, you may choose to recite a mantra during this meditation. A suitable mantra for this practice might be "Om Kali Ma," invoking the goddess Kali as the embodiment of creation and destruction. As you recite the mantra, visualize the goddess guiding you through the process of ego dissolution and spiritual rebirth.

7. **Reflection:**
After 15-20 minutes of meditation, take a moment to reflect on the experience.

Consider how the awareness of death and impermanence can help you live more fully and authentically, free from the attachments and fears of the ego. Reflect on how you can apply these insights to your daily life, making choices that align with the impermanent nature of existence.

8. **Closing:**
   Open your eyes and take a few deep breaths, feeling grounded in the present moment. If you made an offering at the beginning of the meditation, express your gratitude to the earth before you leave. Carry the awareness of impermanence with you as a reminder to live each day with intention, presence, and gratitude.

9. **Optional Extension:**
   To deepen this practice, consider incorporating it into your regular spiritual routine. You can also explore variations of this meditation by focusing on different aspects of impermanence, such as the changing seasons, the life cycle of plants, or the aging process.

10. **Group Practice (Optional):**
    If you have a group of like-minded practitioners, consider conducting a group smashan meditation in a natural setting. Each participant can share their reflections

afterward, fostering a deeper collective understanding of impermanence and spiritual growth.

4. The Kali Devotion Ritual

Purpose:

To honor and connect with the goddess Kali, seeking her guidance and protection on the path to spiritual liberation. This ritual deepens the practitioner's relationship with Kali, the dark mother who embodies both creation and destruction.

Materials:

- A small altar or sacred space
- An image or statue of Kali
- Offerings (flowers, incense, fruits, or sweets)
- A bell or chime
- Red or black cloth (to symbolize Kali's energy)
- A small bowl of water (for purification)

Instructions:

1. **Preparation:**
   Set up your altar or sacred space with an image or statue of Kali at the center. Drape the red or black cloth over the altar to symbolize Kali's powerful energy. Arrange your offerings around the image, and light incense to purify the space. Place the bowl of water on the altar for later use.

2. **Invocation:**
Ring the bell or chime to begin the ritual. Stand or kneel before the altar and offer a prayer to Kali, inviting her presence into the space. You may use the following invocation or create your own: "O Kali Ma, Dark Mother of creation and destruction, I invite you into this space. Guide me on the path to liberation, and protect me from all harm."

3. **Offerings:**
Present your offerings to Kali, placing them on the altar one by one. As you do, express your devotion and gratitude, asking for her blessings and guidance. You may say: "I offer these flowers/sweets/incense to you, Kali Ma, as a token of my love and devotion. Grant me your wisdom, strength, and protection."

4. **Meditation:**
Sit quietly before the altar, gazing at the image of Kali. Visualize her fierce and loving presence surrounding you, her energy filling you with courage and resolve. Meditate on her attributes—her power to destroy the ego, her role as the mother of all beings, and her ability to guide you through the darkest aspects of your spiritual journey.

5. **Purification:**

Dip your fingers into the bowl of water and touch your forehead, heart, and abdomen, symbolizing the purification of your thoughts, emotions, and instincts. As you do, say, "Kali Ma, purify me. Prepare me for the path of liberation." Feel the water cleansing and renewing your energy, making you receptive to Kali's guidance.

6. **Affirmation:**
   As you meditate, repeat the following affirmation silently or aloud: "Kali Ma, I surrender to your will. Guide me, protect me, and lead me to liberation." Feel her energy filling you with strength and determination. Imagine her standing beside you, offering her sword to cut through the illusions and obstacles on your path.

7. **Invocation of the Goddess:**
   If you feel called, you may invoke Kali more deeply into your being. Stand before the altar, and with hands raised, chant her name or a mantra associated with her (e.g., "Om Krim Kali Ma"). As you chant, visualize Kali's energy descending into your body, filling you with her power. Feel her presence merging with your own, empowering you to face any challenges with fearlessness.

8. **Reflection:**

After the meditation and invocation, take a moment to reflect on the experience. Consider how Kali's energy and guidance can assist you in your spiritual journey. Reflect on any insights or messages you received during the ritual, and how you can apply them to your life.

9. **Devotional Offering:**
   As a final act of devotion, consider leaving an offering at a natural site, such as a tree, river, or rock, as a gift to Kali. This offering symbolizes your commitment to honoring her and following her guidance. As you place the offering, silently express your gratitude and devotion.

10. **Closing:**
    Ring the bell or chime again to close the ritual. Thank Kali for her presence and blessings, and extinguish the incense. Leave the offerings on the altar as a sign of your devotion, and carry the energy of the ritual with you throughout your day.

11. **Ongoing Devotion:**
    Consider setting aside regular times to honor Kali, perhaps on a weekly or monthly basis. Over time, this practice can deepen your connection with her and enhance your spiritual journey.

12. **Group Practice (Optional):**
    If you are part of a spiritual group,

consider conducting a group Kali devotion ritual. Each participant can offer their own prayers and reflections, creating a powerful collective energy that honors the goddess and strengthens the bonds within the group.

ANNOTATED BIBLIOGRAPHY FOR FURTHER READING

1. *The Book of the Law* **by Aleister Crowley**

A foundational text in Thelema, *The Book of the Law* presents the core tenets of Crowley's philosophy, emphasizing the concepts of true will, self-deification, and spiritual sovereignty. Crowley's writings have had a significant influence on modern Luciferianism, particularly in their emphasis on personal empowerment and the rejection of external authority.

2. *Luciferian Witchcraft* **by Michael W. Ford**

This comprehensive guide to Luciferianism offers practical rituals, meditations, and philosophical insights for those on the left-hand path. Ford explores the symbolism of Lucifer, the black flame, and the integration of the shadow, providing a valuable resource for practitioners seeking to deepen their understanding of Luciferian spirituality.

3. *Aghora: At the Left Hand of God* by Robert E. Svoboda

A detailed exploration of the Aghora tradition, this book provides a firsthand account of the practices, rituals, and philosophy of the Aghoris. Svoboda's work offers a rare glimpse into the life of an Aghori and the transformative power of confronting death, impurity, and the profane on the path to spiritual liberation.

4. *The Dark Night of the Soul* by St. John of the Cross

Although rooted in Christian mysticism, *The Dark Night of the Soul* explores the concept of ego death and the profound transformation that occurs when the soul undergoes a period of intense spiritual purification. This text is relevant to those studying the parallels between the dark night and the alchemical *nigredo* stage in other traditions.

5. *The Serpent and the Rainbow* by Wade Davis

This anthropological work explores the role of ritual, magic, and spirituality in Haitian Vodou, with a focus on the themes of death and rebirth. While not directly related to Aghora or Luciferianism, it offers valuable insights into the universal aspects of the left-hand path and the transformative power of confronting the shadow.

6. *Prometheus Rising* by Robert Anton Wilson

Wilson's work explores the psychology of human consciousness, the potential for self-transformation, and the role of belief systems in shaping reality. *Prometheus Rising* is a thought-provoking read for those interested in the intersection of psychology, spirituality, and the left-hand path.

7. *Kali: The Black Goddess of Dakshineswar* by Elizabeth U. Harding

This book offers an in-depth exploration of the goddess Kali, her symbolism, and her worship in Hinduism. Harding provides a comprehensive overview of Kali's role in spiritual transformation, making it a valuable resource for those interested in Aghora and the worship of the dark mother.

8. *Jung and the Alchemical Imagination* by Jeffrey Raff

Raff explores the connection between Jungian psychology and alchemical symbolism, offering insights into the processes of shadow integration, ego death, and spiritual rebirth. This book is essential for those interested in the psychological aspects of spiritual alchemy within the context of both Luciferianism and Aghora.

9. *The Yoga of Power: Tantra, Shakti, and the Secret Way* by Julius Evola

Evola's exploration of Tantric practices, including those aligned with the left-hand path, provides a deep understanding of the spiritual techniques used to transcend the ego and achieve spiritual sovereignty. His writings offer a bridge between Eastern and Western esoteric traditions, relevant to both Aghora and Luciferianism.

10. *The Satanic Bible* by Anton LaVey

Though distinct from traditional Luciferianism, *The Satanic Bible* provides an introduction to the philosophy of Satanism, emphasizing personal empowerment, rebellion against external authority, and the celebration of the self. LaVey's work has influenced modern left-hand path practices and offers insights into the broader context of spiritual sovereignty.

GLOSSARY OF TERMS

This expanded glossary includes a broad range of terms relevant to Luciferianism, Aghora, and the left-hand path, providing a comprehensive understanding of the key concepts and practices.

Adept:
A person who has attained a high level of proficiency and understanding in esoteric or occult practices.

Adversary:
In Luciferianism, the Adversary represents the force that opposes the status quo, challenges conformity, and encourages self-empowerment and the pursuit of knowledge.

Advaita:
A Sanskrit term meaning "non-duality." It is a key philosophical concept in Hinduism, particularly in the Aghora tradition, where it signifies the belief that all distinctions between self and other, life and

death, sacred and profane, are ultimately illusory.

Agni:
The Hindu god of fire, often invoked in rituals for purification and transformation. Agni is significant in both Vedic and Tantric traditions.

Ahimsa:
The principle of non-violence, common in Hindu, Buddhist, and Jain traditions. While Aghoris may challenge conventional interpretations of ahimsa, it remains a foundational concept in many spiritual practices.

Astral Projection:
A practice in which the practitioner consciously leaves their physical body to explore the astral plane, a non-physical realm of existence. It is a common practice in many occult traditions, including Luciferianism.

Asura:
In Hindu mythology, asuras are a group of power-seeking deities, often in opposition to the devas (gods). They are sometimes seen as representing the darker, more rebellious aspects of the divine.

Banishing Ritual:
A ritual performed to clear a space of negative or unwanted energies. Banishing rituals are commonly used in both Luciferian and other occult practices.

Bhakti:
A form of devotional worship in Hinduism, often characterized by intense devotion and love for a deity. While not central to Aghora, aspects of bhakti may be integrated into personal practice.

Bija Mantra:
Seed mantras, or single-syllable sounds, believed to have powerful spiritual effects. Common in Tantric practices, these mantras are used to invoke specific energies or deities.

Bodhi:
A term meaning "awakening" or "enlightenment" in Buddhism. It represents the state of awareness and understanding that frees one from the cycle of rebirth.

Chaos Magick:
A modern form of magick that emphasizes the use of belief as a tool for achieving desired outcomes. Practitioners of chaos magick often adopt and discard belief systems at will, reflecting the fluid and adaptable nature of this approach.

Chod:
A Tantric Buddhist practice in which the practitioner symbolically offers their body as a feast to demons and deities. It is a form of cutting through ego attachment and fear.

Daath:

In Kabbalistic mysticism, Daath represents the "hidden" sephira on the Tree of Life. It is associated with knowledge and the abyss that separates the higher and lower aspects of consciousness.

Deification:
The process of becoming godlike, often through spiritual practices that elevate the practitioner to a state of divine awareness and power. Deification is a central goal in Luciferianism.

Dharmic Path:
The path of righteousness and duty in Hinduism. Aghora is often seen as a counterbalance to the Dharmic path, embracing aspects of life that are typically rejected in conventional spiritual practices.

Dhyana:
A state of deep meditation in Hindu and Buddhist traditions. It is the seventh limb of the eightfold path of yoga, leading to Samadhi, or union with the divine.

Doppelgänger:
A shadowy double or counterpart of a living person. In esoteric traditions, encountering one's doppelgänger can be a powerful symbol of facing the shadow self.

Draconian Current:
A term used in some left-hand path practices to

describe the spiritual energy associated with the dragon, a symbol of primordial power, chaos, and transformation.

Egregore:
A collective thoughtform or entity created by the combined energy and intention of a group. Egregores can become powerful spiritual forces, influencing the thoughts and actions of those connected to them.

Ego Death:
The dissolution of the ego, or the sense of separate self, often experienced as a profound transformation in spiritual practice. It is seen as a necessary step towards spiritual enlightenment in many esoteric traditions.

Empowerment Ritual:
A ritual designed to increase personal power, confidence, and spiritual authority. Such rituals are common in Luciferian and other occult practices.

Gnosis:
A term meaning "knowledge" in Greek, often referring to spiritual or mystical insight. Gnosis is a key concept in many esoteric traditions, including Gnosticism and Luciferianism.

Grimoire:
A book of magical knowledge, containing spells, rituals, and instructions for summoning spirits.

Grimoires are central to many occult traditions.

Guru:
A spiritual teacher or guide in Hinduism and Buddhism. In Aghora, the relationship with the guru is crucial for spiritual advancement and the transmission of esoteric knowledge.

Homa/Havan:
A fire ritual in Hinduism, often involving the offering of grains, ghee, and other substances into the sacred fire. These rituals are acts of devotion and purification.

Invocation:
The act of calling upon a deity, spirit, or other supernatural force during a ritual. Invocation is a central practice in both Luciferian and Aghora traditions.

Kaivalya:
A term in Hindu philosophy that means isolation or liberation. It represents the state of absolute independence and freedom from the cycles of birth and death.

Kali Yuga:
The last of the four stages the world goes through as part of the cycle of yugas, or ages, in Hindu cosmology. The Kali Yuga is often associated with moral decline and spiritual darkness.

Karma:

The law of cause and effect in Hinduism and Buddhism, where one's actions determine future experiences. While karma is traditionally seen as a force for maintaining moral order, Aghoris seek to transcend karma through their practices.

Kundalini:

A form of divine feminine energy believed to be coiled at the base of the spine. When awakened, Kundalini energy rises through the chakras, leading to spiritual enlightenment.

Left-Hand Path:

A term used to describe spiritual practices that embrace what is traditionally seen as taboo, forbidden, or oppositional. The left-hand path often involves the pursuit of personal empowerment, rebellion against societal norms, and the integration of the shadow.

Liber AL vel Legis:

Also known as *The Book of the Law*, this is the central sacred text of Thelema, written by Aleister Crowley. It forms the basis of Thelemic philosophy, which emphasizes the pursuit of one's true will.

Lila:

A Sanskrit term meaning "divine play," which refers to the spontaneous, creative, and playful nature of the universe, as well as the actions of the divine. In some traditions, life itself is considered a manifestation of Lila.

Lucifer:
In Luciferianism, Lucifer is the light-bringer, the morning star, and a symbol of enlightenment, rebellion, and self-sovereignty. Lucifer is not seen as an evil figure but as a guide to spiritual empowerment.

Lunar Magic:
Magical practices that are associated with the moon and its cycles. Lunar magic often involves rituals for intuition, emotional healing, and inner transformation.

Mala:
A string of prayer beads used in Hinduism and Buddhism for counting mantras or prayers during meditation. Malas are used in various spiritual practices to focus the mind and deepen concentration.

Mandala:
A geometric figure representing the universe in Hindu and Buddhist symbolism. Mandalas are used as a tool for meditation and spiritual focus, often symbolizing the balance and unity of all things.

Mantra:
A sacred word, sound, or phrase repeated in meditation or ritual to focus the mind and invoke spiritual power. Mantras are commonly used in both Hindu and Buddhist practices.

Moksha:
In Hinduism and other Indian religions, moksha refers to the liberation from the cycle of birth, death, and rebirth (samsara). It is the ultimate spiritual goal, representing the soul's release from the bondage of karma and its union with the divine. Moksha is characterized by the realization of one's true nature and the attainment of a state of eternal peace, bliss, and oneness with the absolute reality. In Aghora, moksha is sought through practices that confront and transcend conventional dualities, ultimately leading to spiritual liberation and non-duality.

Mantra:
A sacred word, sound, or phrase repeated in meditation or ritual to focus the mind and invoke spiritual power. Mantras are commonly used in both Hindu and Buddhist practices, and can be tailored to specific intentions, such as invoking deities, enhancing concentration, or purifying the mind.

Mudra:
A symbolic hand gesture used in Hindu and Buddhist rituals and meditations to channel energy and focus the mind. Each mudra is associated with specific spiritual effects, such as protection, healing, or enlightenment.

Necromancy:

A form of magic that involves communication with the dead, typically to gain insight, predict the future, or harness spiritual power. While often seen as a dark art, necromancy can be used for various purposes depending on the tradition.

Nigredo:
In alchemy, the first stage of the alchemical process, also known as the "blackening." It represents the dissolution or breaking down of the self, often associated with confronting the shadow and undergoing intense inner transformation.

Non-Duality:
The philosophical concept that all distinctions between self and other, light and dark, sacred and profane are illusory. Non-duality is the realization of oneness with the divine, a central concept in both Aghora and Luciferianism.

Nyasa:
A Tantric practice in which specific mantras are mentally placed or inscribed on different parts of the body. Nyasa is often used to consecrate the body and align it with spiritual energies or deities.

Occult:
A broad term encompassing esoteric knowledge and practices related to the hidden or unseen aspects of reality. The occult includes a wide range of traditions, such as alchemy, astrology, magic, and mysticism.

Pantheon:
A group of deities worshiped within a particular religious tradition. In Hinduism, for example, the pantheon includes gods like Shiva, Vishnu, and Kali. Luciferianism may also draw upon various mythological figures in its symbolic framework.

Philosopher's Stone:
In alchemy, a legendary substance believed to enable the transmutation of base metals into gold and grant immortality. The Philosopher's Stone is also a metaphor for spiritual enlightenment and the perfection of the soul.

Pranayama:
The practice of breath control in yoga, used to regulate the flow of energy (prana) in the body. Pranayama is an important aspect of both physical and spiritual practices in Hinduism and Buddhism.

Puja:
A ritual of worship in Hinduism, typically involving offerings of food, flowers, incense, and prayers to deities. Puja can be performed daily at home or in a temple, and it serves as a way to honor and connect with the divine.

Reincarnation:
The belief in the rebirth of the soul in a new body after death. Reincarnation is a core concept in Hinduism and Buddhism, where the cycle of

birth, death, and rebirth (samsara) is considered something to transcend through spiritual practice.

Right-Hand Path:
In contrast to the left-hand path, the right-hand path refers to spiritual practices that adhere to societal norms, conventional morality, and often focus on selflessness and devotion. It is often associated with mainstream religious practices.

Ritual:
A series of actions performed in a prescribed order, often imbued with symbolic meaning, to achieve a specific spiritual goal. Rituals can range from simple daily practices to elaborate ceremonies and are central to both Luciferianism and Aghora.

Sadhana:
A disciplined spiritual practice or routine undertaken to achieve spiritual goals. Sadhana may include meditation, mantra recitation, yoga, rituals, and other forms of spiritual work.

Samsara:
The cycle of birth, death, and rebirth that souls undergo in Hinduism and Buddhism. The goal of spiritual practice is to break free from samsara and attain liberation (moksha or nirvana).

Samadhi:
A state of deep, meditative absorption in which the practitioner experiences a sense of unity with the

divine. It is the final limb of the eightfold path in yoga and represents the pinnacle of spiritual practice.

Sephiroth:
In Kabbalistic mysticism, the ten attributes through which the divine manifests in the world. The Sephiroth are depicted on the Tree of Life, a symbolic diagram used in esoteric teachings.

Sigil:
A symbolic representation used in magic to embody a specific intent or desire. Sigils are often created by reducing a statement of intent into a unique symbol and then charging it with energy through ritual.

Tantra:
A spiritual tradition within Hinduism and Buddhism that focuses on the use of rituals, mantras, and meditative practices to achieve spiritual enlightenment. Tantra emphasizes the unity of opposites and often involves the integration of sacred and profane elements.

Tattvas:
The five basic elements in Hindu and Buddhist metaphysics: earth, water, fire, air, and ether (space). These elements are considered the building blocks of the material and spiritual worlds.

Thelema:

A spiritual philosophy developed by Aleister Crowley, centered on the principle of "Do what thou wilt shall be the whole of the Law." Thelema emphasizes the pursuit of one's true will and is closely associated with occult practices.

Tree of Life:

A central symbol in Kabbalistic mysticism, representing the structure of the universe and the human soul. The Tree of Life consists of ten sephiroth and twenty-two paths, each corresponding to different aspects of creation and spiritual development.

True Will:

In Thelema and other esoteric traditions, true will refers to the individual's innermost purpose or divine mission in life. Discovering and aligning with one's true will is considered essential for spiritual fulfillment.

Upaya:

A concept in Buddhism meaning "skillful means" or "expedient methods." Upaya refers to the various practices and teachings that can be employed to lead beings to enlightenment, tailored to their specific needs and capacities.

Vama Marg:

The left-hand path in Tantric practices, often associated with non-conventional and sometimes taboo practices aimed at transcending social norms and achieving spiritual liberation.

Vibration:
In occult practices, vibration refers to the chanting or intonation of words or mantras with focused intent to alter consciousness or invoke spiritual energies. Vibrations are often used in rituals to amplify the power of the words spoken.

Yantra:
A geometric diagram used in Hindu and Buddhist meditation practices. Yantras are visual tools that represent different aspects of the divine and are used to focus the mind during meditation.

Yogi/Yogini:
A practitioner of yoga, often someone who has dedicated their life to spiritual practice. A yogi (male) or yogini (female) seeks to achieve union with the divine through disciplines such as meditation, pranayama, and ethical living.

Zazen:
A form of seated meditation practiced in Zen Buddhism. Zazen involves focusing on the breath and maintaining a posture of mindfulness, with the goal of achieving a state of pure awareness and insight.

Also Available From Mokshadas Press

✼ ✼ ✼

Lucifer's Library
Occult Wisdom Through The Ages

The Luciferian Epic
Poems of Rebellion & Redemption

ShadowLight
Integrating Luciferian Wisdom

Luciferian Meditations
Embracing The Light of The Morning Star

Lucifer in Art
Beauty, Rebellion, and Redemption

Printed in Great Britain
by Amazon